ENCYCLOPEDIA OF MAMMALS

VOLUME 7
Ham–Hye

MARSHALL CAVENDISH
NEW YORK • LONDON • TORONTO • SYDNEY

HAMSTERS

RELATIONS

Hamsters and dormice belong to the order Rodentia, which comprises thirty families of rodent. Other species are:

BEAVERS

SQUIRRELS

RATS

MICE

CAVIES

GOPHERS

R. Cramm GDT/Bruce Coleman Ltd.

Hamsters and dormice belong to the order Rodentia. Rodents are divided into three sub-orders, based on the structure of their skulls and the muscles of their jaws. The three suborders are Sciuromorpha (squirrel-like rodents), Myomorpha (mouselike rodents), and Caviomorpha (cavylike rodents). Dormice and hamsters belong to the myomorphs, or mouselike rodents.

ORDER

Rodentia
(rodents)

SUBORDER

Myomorpha

DORMOUSE FAMILIES

*Gliridae
Seleviniidae*

EIGHT GENERA

The family Gliridae contains seven genera

ELEVEN SPECIES

HAMSTER FAMILY

Muridae

SUBFAMILY

Cricetinae
(hamsters)

GENERA

five

SPECIES

twenty-four

BUILDERS AND BURROWERS

HAMSTERS AND DORMICE HAVE PROVED THEMSELVES TO BE HIGHLY ADAPTABLE CREATURES, ABLE TO SURVIVE IN EXTREME CLIMATES AND REGIONS RANGING FROM ROCKY TERRAINS TO GRASSY LOWLAND HILLS

Rodents belong to the most successful order of mammals. With over 1,700 species they make up well over 40 percent of all mammals. The order, Rodentia, is also a highly diverse group of animals. They include mammals as varied as porcupines, beavers, chinchillas, squirrels, and, of course, rats and mice.

Rodents are found almost everywhere in the world. Their ability to adapt quickly to new environmental challenges makes them the widest ranging of all mammal orders. In fact, only humans have a greater range. Some rodents, like the hamster, have evolved specialized characteristics that help them in their underground existence, while other species of rodent prefer to live above ground. Other rodents, such as dormice, are more generalized in their characteristics, enabling them to alternate between life on the ground and life high in the trees. Among the many features that have contributed to

913

the success of the rodents, few are as important as their characteristic teeth and jaws. With powerful jaw muscles and tough, self-sharpening teeth, rodents are able to chew their way through almost anything, from the hard shells of nuts to wood, and even man-made materials such as plastic and sheet metal. Although some rodents have specialized diets, most are able to adapt to whatever is available. This gives them an advantage over other mammals, as well as an almost inexhaustible food supply. It is this feature, coupled with their ability to produce large numbers of offspring, that has made them so successful.

The rodents have a long evolutionary history and were among the first mammals to appear.

THE TINY JAPANESE PYGMY DORMOUSE HAS A HEAD-AND-BODY LENGTH OF ONLY 2.5 IN (64 MM)

Their fossil remains have been found in rocks that are over sixty million years old and date from the Paleocene period—soon after the dinosaurs became extinct. The ancestral rodents were squirrel-like creatures. One of the first to appear was *Paramys* (PAR-a-miss)—meaning "near mouse."

These early rodents, which came from North America, were large animals with bodies nearly 23 in (58 cm) long. They also had long tails that were probably covered in thick fur like modern-day squirrels. Their claws were fairly long and curved.

Golden, or Syrian, hamsters (right) *make good pets and are popular with children in the west.*

The Chinese hamster (below) *makes up one of the twelve species of ratlike hamsters.*

A dormouse of west Africa (above) *scuttles up a branch of a cocoa tree.*

Paramys would have used these claws to climb about in the trees.

With the extinction of the dinosaurs a number of ecological niches were left vacant that had been filled by many different groups of mammals. Over the next ten million years the number of rodent species exploded as they began to out-compete

THE FIRST HAMSTERS PROBABLY ORIGINATED IN EASTERN EUROPE OR WESTERN ASIA

other, less successful mammal groups. During the Miocene period (about 23 million years ago) rodents evolved into several remarkable creatures, some of which grew to enormous sizes.

The rodents spread throughout all the continents of the world, except Antarctica, and quickly dominated a wide variety of habitats, including deserts, forests, and swamps. Although they varied in size, many recognizable species appeared early on. Indeed, one species of dormouse that appeared during the Pleistocene period some one and a half million years ago, called *Leithia* (LEE-thee-a), was virtually indistinguishable from modern-day dormice except for its much larger size. It grew to about 10 in (25 cm) long, excluding its tail. This is probably due to the fact that it lived on the Mediterranean islands of Sardinia and Malta, and had few natural predators. Because it did not need to hide from enemies, *Leithia* grew quite large.

Myomorphs, the suborder that includes dormice and hamsters, as well as rats and mice, evolved in the Eocene period, between 50 and 40 million years ago. These highly adaptable creatures soon filled virtually all available habitats, including that of the ever-increasing human population.

As with all rodents, the teeth of dormice and hamsters are particularly well suited to their lifestyle. All rodents have two pairs of large, sharp front teeth—incisor teeth—which continue to grow throughout the animal's life. The rodent must gnaw on hard substances to wear these teeth down and

---

ONE RODENT, TELICOMYS, WHICH EVOLVED DURING THE MIOCENE PERIOD, WAS OVER 6 FT (1.8 M) LONG

---

stop them from growing too long. In captivity it is very important to give rodents wood and nutshells to gnaw on or their teeth will grow so long that they cannot open their mouths wide enough to get food in and they will eventually starve to death.

Directly behind these teeth is a gap called the *diastema* (DIE-a-stee-ma). Many rodents have a flap of skin on the side of their heads that they are able to draw into this gap. Others have distinctive cheek pouches, allowing them to carry huge quantities of food to store in their burrows or nests for times of shortage. Behind the diastemata are between four and ten cheek teeth, which are used for grinding hard, dry food before swallowing. ∎

CHEEK POUCHES

Hamsters' cheek pouches can be filled with food, which can then be carried back and stored in the underground burrow. The pouches can hold a remarkable quantity of food. In some types of hamster, they can stretch wide enough to hold an amount of food equivalent to about half the size of the hamster itself.

Hamsters also use their pouches to carry their nesting material, and occasionally as floats when swimming. When full, the cheek pouches extend back beyond the level of the animal's shoulder blades.

COMMON EUROPEAN HAMSTER
Cricetus cricetus
(*cry-SEAT-uss cry-SEAT-uss*)

This species is found in central Europe and Russia. It is one of twenty-four species of hamster in the subfamily Cricetinae, within the Muridae family.

RATS AND MIC

SQUIRREL-LIKE RODENTS

Hamsters and dormice belong to the rodent suborder Myomorpha, which also includes mice, rats, voles, gerbils, lemmings, and jerboas. There are over a thousand species in the suborder and these are classified in five families and 264 genera. The most important and largest family is the Muridae (rats and mice).

DORMICE

GLIRIDAE   SELEVINIIDAE

JERBOAS

JUMPING MICE

FAT DORMOUSE

Also known as the edible dormouse, this dormouse is one of the ten species in the Gliridae family. The family Seleviniidae contains only one species.

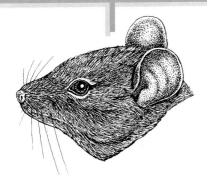

MOUSELIKE
RODENTS

CAVYLIKE
RODENTS

All illustrations Evi Antoniou

917

RODENTS

ANATOMY:
THE HAMSTER

The smallest hamster is the Dzungarian dwarf hamster at 2–4 in (5.1–10.2 cm). The largest is the common or black-bellied hamster (above left) at 7.8–11 in (20–28 cm). Dormice (above center) range in size from 2.5 in (6.4 cm) to 7.5 in (19 cm). They are compared with a house mouse (above right).

FOOT PATTERNS

Hamsters and dormice have four digits on the front feet and five on the back. In both species the front paws are extremely dexterous.

OTHER FOOT PATTERNS

Some rodents have four digits on both front and back feet. These include rock rats and gundis.

EYES

Although hamsters have large eyes, their eyesight is poor. They are burrowers that spend most of the day underground where they rely more on their keen sense of smell.

PAWS AND CLAWS

The paws of the front legs are modified hands, giving greater dexterity in the manipulation of food. Hamsters use a characteristic squeezing movement when emptying their pouches.

Hands & feet illustration Elisabeth Smith

Main illustration & sizes Simon Turvey/Wildlife Art Agency

X
R
A
Y

THE HAMSTER SKELETON

The skeleton of the hamster shows a thick-set body and strong hind leg bones, which support the hamster when sitting up during feeding. The shorter forelimbs facilitate burrowing, foraging, and climbing.

SHORT FORELIMBS

FIVE DIGITS ON HIND FEET

SHORT STUMPY TAIL

Molar teeth have protuberances that always occur in two parallel, longitudinal lines.

X-ray illustrations Elisabeth Smith

EARS

Hamsters have acute hearing and communicate with ultrasounds as well as with squeaks audible to the human ear.

SCENT GLANDS

Territories are marked with secretions from scent glands. Hamsters also rely on scent to tell them when the females are in heat.

TAIL

The tail is short, or no more than a stump. This suits the hamster's burrowing lifestyle. A long, bushy tail would attract damp soil.

CLASSIFICATION

GENUS: *CRICETUS*

SPECIES: *CRICETUS*

SIZE

HEAD AND BODY: 8–13 IN (20–33 CM)

TAIL: 1.5–2.4 IN (3.8–6.1 CM)

WEIGHT: 4–32 OZ (113–907 G)

WEIGHT AT BIRTH: 0.3 OZ (8.5 G)

COLORATION

REDDISH- AND YELLOW-COLORED FUR WITH A BLACK UNDERBELLY. USUALLY HAS WHITE ON SIDES, MUZZLE, AND PAWS

FEATURES

BRIGHT, BEADY EYES

SMALL, ROUNDED, FUR-COVERED EARS

COMMON DORMOUSE

CLASSIFICATION

GENUS: *MUSCARDINUS*

SPECIES: *AVELLANARIUS*

SIZE

HEAD AND BODY: 2.4–3.5 IN (6–9 CM)

TAIL: 2–3 IN (5.1–7.6 CM)

WEIGHT: 0.5–1.5 OZ (14.2–42.5 G)

WEIGHT AT BIRTH: 0.4–0.5 OZ (11.3–14.2 G)

COLORATION

RICH, GOLDEN-COLORED COAT ON BACK. THE THROAT AND CHEST ARE CREAMY WHITE AND ITS BELLY IS PINKISH BUFF

FEATURES

BRIGHT, BEADY, BLACK EYES

SMALL, ROUNDED EARS

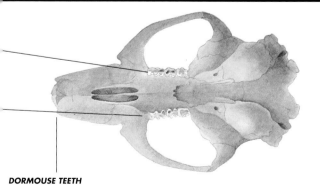

DORMOUSE TEETH

Hamsters have developed very strong jaws because much of their diet consists of nuts and seeds that have to be cracked open. This also equips them with a fierce bite for use in aggressive confrontations. Prominent incisors and premolars extend along the outside of the lower jaw.

UPPER AND LOWER JAWS OF A HAMSTER

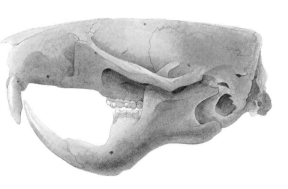

SILENT FORAGERS

SLEEPY AND SECRETIVE, BOTH DORMICE AND HAMSTERS ARE VERY SELDOM SEEN DURING THE HOURS OF DAYLIGHT, AND ARE ONLY ACTIVE AT DUSK AND AT DAWN WHEN THEY CAN AVOID MOST PREDATORS

Hamsters build extensive burrows that are usually between 19.6–39 in (50–100 cm) below the ground. However, burrows have been found that go down to nearly three times this depth. The number and type of the entrance holes depend on the age and sex of the hamster. Both males and females will have vertical tunnels and more gradually sloping ones. Female hamsters usually have several more entrances than the males. Each burrow is divided up into special storage chambers and living areas. The way the burrow is constructed depends on the age and sex of the animal using it.

> **STARTLED HAMSTERS HAVE BEEN KNOWN TO JUMP OVER 3.2 FT (1 M) IN THE AIR**

Male hamsters tend to build burrows with many storage chambers for food, while females concentrate on their main living chamber, lining it with fine grasses to keep it warm and snug, as this is where she will give birth and look after her litter. All hamster burrows also have a chamber set aside as a lavatory. As a general rule, the more complex the burrow, the older the hamster.

VICIOUS FIGHTS

Sometimes, when there is plenty of food in a certain area, or if there are not enough places to dig burrows, large numbers of hamsters will gather together in a small area, creating the impression that hamsters are communal animals, happily living alongside one another. This is not true. Hamsters are solitary by nature, and avoid contact with others, except during the mating season, which occurs from midspring to summer. If they meet outside this time, they will fight viciously, and can inflict serious injuries. However, in captivity they lose much of this aggressiveness.

Unlike hamsters, which are burrowers, dormice spend most of their lives in trees and shrubs. Dormice are nocturnal and spend the entire day fast asleep in nests that are woven from grasses and bark that is stripped from shrubs and trees. Their nests may be anywhere from 39 in (100 cm) below the ground to high in the trunk of some mature trees about 65.6 ft (20 m) above the ground.

Dormice are active at night, foraging for food at the tops of trees and bushes. They eat mainly plant

The garden dormouse, Eliomys quercinus, *(right).*

The common dormouse (right) *lives in thickets and areas of secondary growth in forests.*

George McCarthy/Bruce Coleman Ltd.

The fat or edible dormouse (above). *This squirrel-like rodent lives in trees, but also builds burrows.*

matter, enjoying all kinds of fruit, seeds, flowers, buds, acorns, and nuts. The common dormouse is so fond of hazelnuts that in some parts of the world it is known as the hazel dormouse. Dormice also eat insects and occasionally nestling birds. Like that of many rodents, a dormouse's diet also consists of various kinds of plant material, such as fruit, seeds, and buds. This variety endows them broad adaptability.

Dormice have an acute sense of hearing, and their large eyes enable them to see well in the dark.

COMMON HAMSTERS IN CAPTIVITY MUST BE HANDLED CAREFULLY AS THEIR SHARP TEETH CAN INFLICT A PAINFUL WOUND

They are agile climbers and spend most of their lives among the trees and bushes, rarely, if ever, coming down to the ground where they are more vulnerable to predators. They have long, furry tails that they use for several purposes. While up in the trees, the tail acts as a counterbalance as they scamper through the branches. Partially wrapped around their bodies it breaks up their body shape, making it more difficult for enemies to spot them while foraging. The tail also helps them to keep warm. While sleeping, dormice curl their tails around themselves, helping to insulate their bodies against the cold at night and during hibernation. ∎

HABITATS

The first hamsters probably originated in eastern Europe or western Asia. With the arrival of humans they were able to follow the spread of agriculture across Europe, as far west as Belgium and east into Russia. Although improved and mechanized farming methods are now destroying much of their natural habitats, hamsters are prolific breeders, and their survival is not yet threatened.

Hamsters generally live in areas with plenty of dry, sandy soil or clay, which they can dig through without too much effort. They often dig their runways through the complex systems of meadow plants' roots, ensuring greater stability. Hamsters

---

LIKE MANY RODENTS, FEMALE HAMSTERS WILL EAT YOUNG THAT DO NOT SURVIVE

---

are also found in grassy and cultivated land, and on lowland hills where they can survive at altitudes of over 1,968 ft (600 m).

Common hamsters were once found in abundance throughout central Europe, as well as parts of the former USSR. However, improved agricultural techniques that can damage and destroy their burrows, as well as the increasing need for more land to grow crops, have significantly reduced their numbers. Fortunately, they are still

Raimund Cramm GDT/Bruce Coleman Ltd.

The common hamster (above) was once plentiful throughout central Europe.

P. Morris

Dormice (left) are agile climbers and spend most of their time in the branches of trees.

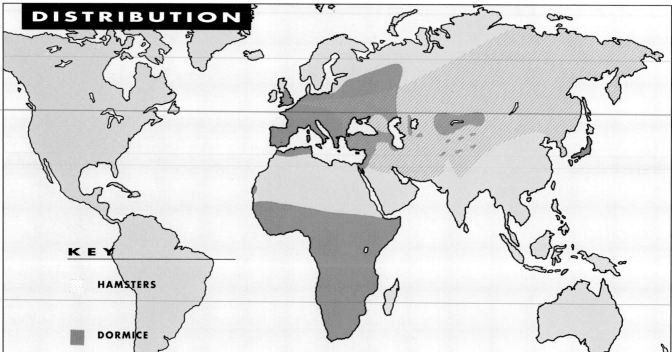

DISTRIBUTION

KEY

HAMSTERS

DORMICE

THE HAMSTER'S BURROW

Characteristics vary from species to species. Food supplies are usually stored in dead-end tunnels or widened areas. Some hamsters will build several food-storage burrows separate from their main living quarters. The amount of food stored also varies. Striped hamsters store about 7 oz (200 g), while migratory hamsters store 14–18 oz (400–500 g). Some species of ratlike hamsters take in large amounts of winter supplies, such as potatoes and soybeans that have been looted from nearby farms.

Angela Hargreaves/Wildlife Art Agency

KEY FACTS

● Hamsters belong to the largest order of mammals—the rodents. In total, there are nearly 2,000 separate species in this order, including lemmings, rats, voles, and gerbils.

● Despite the fact that they are called fat dormice, these athletic creatures are able to leap distances of up to 33 ft (10 m). The fat dormouse was introduced to England in 1902 by Lord Rothschild.

● During mating, common hamsters can emit high-pitched squeaks that cannot be heard by humans.

● A small number of golden hamsters were brought into the United States as laboratory animals in 1938, and by 1950 it was estimated that there were over 100,000 of them kept as pets.

● When hibernating, dormice sleep so soundly that they can be picked up and rolled across a table without waking up. This feature earned them their name from the French or Latin *dormire*, which means to sleep.

able to thrive in pastures, steppes, and along riverbanks. One naturalist noted how the common hamster was abundant in fields of lucerne in central Germany. This was because lucerne grows rapidly—within eight to ten days after the last crop has been mowed, a new crop has already become thick, providing the hamsters with constant cover. Lucerne also grows in dry habitats, and its green plant material is particularly rich in vitamins and minerals, so the hamsters can take advantage of a nourishing supply of food in autumn and spring when food is lacking in other fields. Plots of lucerne were found to have three times as many burrows as did neighboring fields of grain.

Other hamsters, on the other hand, remain true mountain animals, frequenting dry areas at the foot of mountains up to heights of 13,124–16,494 ft (4,000–5,000 m) and in belts of evergreen trees. Like most other hamsters, they avoid moist areas and areas built up by man. One exception is the Chinese ratlike hamster, which has been found living near moist meadow bogs.

Golden hamsters, which frequent desert regions (see right) where water is scarce, are able to survive by drinking tiny droplets of dew that form in the early morning. With the variation in temperature, some moisture from the air collects as dew, even when there is no rain. This is supplemented by what little moisture they get from their food.

Another species that is found in semidesert regions is the dwarf hamster, which has a particularly

---

IN MANY FARMING REGIONS HAMSTERS ARE REGARDED AS PESTS BECAUSE OF THE DAMAGE THEY CAUSE TO CROPS

---

good camouflage coloring that helps it blend in with the desert.

TERRAIN

The type of terrain often dictates how burrows are built. In central Europe, hibernating hamsters usually dig burrows in flat fields, keeping a good distance between each one. In some foothill regions of Asia, however, hamsters have been observed building burrows in groups on southeasterly slopes. The dense crowding is not due to a tendency to live

together in colonies, but to the limited number of sites suitable for burrow construction.

The natural habitat for dormice is in mature forests and rocky places. However, several species have been able to adapt to life in parks and gardens. They are found in most of Europe, through Asia, and into Russia. Dormice are becoming increasingly rare in the wild as their woodland homes are destroyed by deforestation. Some species, however, have benefited from human encroachment, stealing stored apples, plums, and other varieties of nourishing fruit. ∎

FOCUS ON

THE SYRIAN DESERT

Hamsters are remarkably adaptable animals, capable of living in extreme conditions. The golden hamster has adapted to life in the Syrian Desert. As in all desert habitats, temperatures vary widely from day to night and the hamster must be able to cope with both the extreme heat of the desert sun and the dramatic drop in temperature at night.

During the day, golden hamsters avoid the extreme heat by sleeping in their burrows. They dig down to a depth of about 39 in (99 cm), insulating themselves against the high surface temperatures. In this way they avoid dehydrating in the heat of the day.

In the desert, nighttime temperatures fall dramatically as there is no cloud cover to keep the heat in. As the temperature drops in the evening, golden hamsters emerge from their burrows to search for food. Here, once again, the desert is an inhospitable place and food supplies are scarce. The golden hamster's main diet consists of dry seeds that it sifts from the desert soil. It supplements its diet with green plants, whenever these are available, and may also feed on insects.

Hamsters travel long distances at night, gathering food in their cheek pouches for storage in their burrow. By storing food in times of relative plenty, golden hamsters are able to regulate their food supply.

Gunter Heil/ZEFA

TEMPERATURE AND RAINFALL

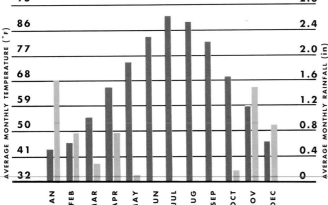

TEMPERATURE
RAINFALL

AVERAGE MONTHLY TEMPERATURE (°F): 95, 86, 77, 68, 59, 50, 41, 32

AVERAGE MONTHLY RAINFALL (in): 2.8, 2.4, 2.0, 1.6, 1.2, 0.8, 0.4, 0

JAN, FEB, MAR, APR, MAY, JUN, JUL, AUG, SEP, OCT, NOV, DEC

Summer temperatures in the Syrian Desert reach an average peak of 91.4°F (33°C) in July. From June to the end of September rainfall is virtually nonexistent.

NEIGHBORS

Hamsters share their desert terrain with a contrasting and colorful assortment of creatures that range from the camel and brown hare to the predatory scorpion.

CAMEL

Camels are supremely well adapted to life in the desert, being able to conserve water and food.

BROWN HARE

This species is related to the jackrabbits of the western United States.

Illustrations Kim Thompson

ENEMIES

SYRIA'S DRY WILDERNESS

The Syrian Desert (Badiet esh Sham) lies to the east of the Ghab Depression, an extension of the Great Rift Valley. The main fertile areas in Syria—where most of the population is concentrated—are the coastal strip and the basin of the River Euphrates.

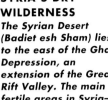

SYRIAN DESERT

EXTREMELY DANGEROUS

GRAY WOLF

The wolf is a social animal and lives in packs. It will dig hamsters out of their burrows.

MODERATELY DANGEROUS

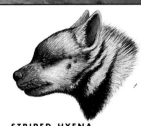

STRIPED HYENA

This mainly nocturnal carnivore lives in northern Africa and southern Asia from Turkey to India.

MODERATELY DANGEROUS

COMMON KESTREL

The kestrel hunts rodents, frogs, and small birds. It hovers in the sky, before diving onto its prey.

FAT-TAILED SCORPION

One of the most venomous scorpions in the world, it feeds on other invertebrates and lizards.

SOUSLIK

This squirrel feeds mainly on seeds, which it carries in its cheek pouches. It hibernates in the winter.

DESERT EAGLE OWL

Found in the northwest part of the North African desert, these birds are small and pale.

MONGOOSE

Most mongooses are carnivorous, but supplement their diet with plant material.

IBEX

Ibexes, wild goats capable of withstanding the harsh environment, can eat the toughest of browse.

FOOD AND FEEDING

Hamsters are mainly herbivorous in their diet, feeding on a wide variety of plant material including leaves, roots, and seeds. They are particularly fond of barley, wheat, millet, soybeans, peas, and root crops such as carrots, sugar beet, and potatoes. This has caused them to be in conflict with humans, particularly in rural areas, where many farmers view hamsters as vermin because of the damage they cause to their crops.

HUNGRY HOARDERS

If the opportunity arises, hamsters will also eat insects, small birds, frogs, lizards, and occasionally snakes. In captivity they thrive on cabbage, lettuce, grain, and dog kibble. Hamsters sit on their hind legs when feeding, using their sensitive, handlike front paws to grasp their food. In times of plenty, especially during the autumn, hamsters gather large quantities of food for storage. They carefully pack their cheek pouches with cereals, seeds, and pulses. They then wedge pieces of roots and leaves behind

Pictures Press-tige/Oxford Scientific Films

HOW THE HAMSTER USES ITS CHEEK POUCHES

NUTCRACKERS

The hamster uses its sharp front teeth for gnawing through nuts.

The hamster's cheek pouches are very elastic and extend back to the shoulders, giving the animal an out-of-shape appearance when full. Although the hamster will eat almost anything, most of its diet consists of plant matter, usually farm products such as corn kernels. Of the live prey it will eat, the hamster prefers earthworms and field mice.

their front teeth, or incisors, and carry them back to the storage chambers.

Once inside the safety of the burrow, hamsters carefully remove the food, using their dexterous forepaws to squeeze the seeds from their cheek pouches. The food is stored in specially designated chambers within the burrow. The roots and leaves are often stored separately from the seeds.

SUPER STORES

Hamsters take their name from the German word *hamstern*, which means "to hoard." On average, hamsters need 26–33 lb (12–15 kg) of food to survive the winter, but many hamsters will store even

Adult female golden hamsters (left) *give off an odor during their estrous cycle to attract males.*

in SIGHT

A FEAST FIT FOR AN EMPEROR

In ancient Rome, the fat dormouse was a culinary delicacy. The rodents were fattened on nuts to make their flesh more flavorsome, then cooked in honey and served with poppy seeds.

Owen Newman/Oxford Scientific Films

BARLEY

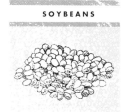

SOYBEANS

PEAS

POTATOES

CARROTS

PACKING THE POUCHES

The hamster carefully packs the cheek pouches with grains, seeds, and pulses, then wedges leaves behind its incisors.

IN THE BURROW

The hamster uses its paws to squeeze out the tightly packed seeds which it then stores.

more than this. Korean gray hamsters from China are some of the most remarkable hoarders. They have been known to store some 60 lb (27 kg) of grain in their burrows. Indeed, during times of war or famine, Chinese peasants have been able to survive by digging up the Korean gray hamsters' stores. Common hamsters are equally enthusiastic, and have been known to store far more food than they could hope to eat. In one instance, the winter food supply was found to contain about 198 lb (90

> THREE FAT DORMICE WERE OBSERVED EATING 270 CHERRIES, 90 PLUMS, 65 APPLES, 40 APRICOTS, 530 GOOSEBERRIES, AND 200 PUMPKIN SEEDS IN JUST 10 DAYS

kg) of roots and seeds, which is the equivalent of nearly 200 times its own body weight.

If the hamster population of a certain area increases too quickly, or there is not enough food to support all the animals, large-scale migrations will occur as the animals search for new homes. They are able to cross most obstacles and, being good swimmers, are able to cross even quite large rivers. They manage this by inflating their large cheek pouches with air to give them greater buoyancy in the water and then paddling furiously to the other side. However, being small animals they are in more danger of freezing to death when wet. ∎

LIFE CYCLE

Hamsters start looking for a mate after emerging from their winter sleep. The mating season lasts from early April until well into August. The male hamsters first have to find the burrow of a female. On finding the female's territory, a male hamster marks the area near the burrow entrance with scent secretions produced from its flank glands. This will warn other males that he is in the area. The male may try to mate with the female by force, but more usually the two hamsters will watch each other nervously, chattering or grinding their teeth. The female may jump around, trying to bite the male, but if she is receptive, she will allow the male to enter her burrow. Once mating is over, the female drives the male out, and reverts to her solitary way of life.

Although the female is capable of producing a litter just about every month, in the wild she usually has just two litters a year. After about 18 to 20 days, the female gives birth to a litter of between

One of the ten species of African dormouse (right), *which is found throughout the forest and savanna zones of Africa.*

IF A PREDATOR SEIZES A DORMOUSE BY ITS TAIL, THE TIP BREAKS OFF, LEAVING THE ATTACKER WITH A MOUTHFUL OF FUR

---

four and twelve young. They are born naked and blind and are very tiny. The young may nibble at grass after about a week, although they are not weaned until they are three weeks old. By the time they are two weeks old, they have a thick coat of fur and have opened their eyes.

As soon as the young are weaned, they leave their mother and have to fend for themselves. Although they are only with their mother for a short space of time, she is extremely caring. If there is any danger, she will move her young quickly to safety by gathering them into her mouth. She will put them into her cheek pouches or carry them in the space between her incisors and the cheek teeth.

Young female hamsters are sexually mature after about sixty days. Because of this high rate of reproductivity, hamsters are in little danger of extinction, even though they have many natural predators, such as polecats, wolves, bears, wildcats, kestrels, and falcons, and, of course, humans.

DORMICE

Like hamsters, dormice awake at the start of spring and start looking for a mate. Some are quite vocal in their search. Male edible dormice may emit high-pitched squeaks as they pursue the females; and

THE DORMOUSE'S DEEP SLEEP

Hibernation is a particularly dangerous time for small mammals. They must store enough fat on their bodies to last the whole winter—even if spring is later than usual. The first winter hibernation is usually the most perilous. Some 40 percent of small mammals fail to wake up after this deep sleep. Hibernating mammals are unable to defend themselves. They rely on their ability to hide and hope that predators will not find them.

Peter Ward/Bruce Coleman Ltd.

Owen Newman/Oxford Scientific Films

female garden dormice whistle to attract males. Male dormice compete ferociously for the right to mate with a female.

After mating, males and females part company, and the males do not take any further part in the rearing of the young. They then spend the rest of the spring searching for other females to mate with. The females build a nest that they line with moss, leaves, hair, and feathers. Usually this nest is built in a hollow tree, fairly near to the ground, and it is bigger than her usual sleeping nest. Sometimes several nests are built close together, and if suitable nesting sites are few and far between, two, and occasionally three, females will share a nest, each rearing its own offspring.

A litter of week-old common dormice (above) *in their nest.*

The adult garden dormouse (below) *is slightly smaller than the fat dormouse.*

After a gestation period of about 19–30 days, the female gives birth to between two and ten young. The young are born naked and blind and are wholly dependent on their mother. She leaves the young in the nest at night while she goes out to feed, but returns periodically to suckle them.

The young get their first fur after about seven days. This is usually gray in color, and molts at about two weeks to give a lighter version of the adult's coloring. Young dormice open their eyes at between 10 and 18 days. They are fully weaned after about one month, but will remain with their mother until they are about two months old. At this point they leave the

Francisco Marquez/Bruce Coleman Ltd.

nest to begin searching for their own accommodation. They remain within a short radius of the maternal nest for the first year. The young are sexually mature after their first hibernation. If the weather is good, the adult female may produce two litters of young each year.

Dormice are quite long lived compared with other small mammals. Some species, such as the garden dormouse, may live for about five years in the wild. In captivity they have been known to live for almost twice this length of time. While fattening up for winter, dormice also reduce their protein intake, which automatically makes them much sleepier than usual. They then find a snug place to nest, usually in the hollow of a tree, fairly close to the ground. After adding a few nuts and seeds, the dormice settle down to their long winter sleep. All dormice sleep curled up, with their tails wrapped around them for extra warmth. They sleep so soundly that hibernating dormice have been known to fall to the ground without even stirring.

AT RISK

All hibernators are at risk if the outside temperature drops too low. At temperatures below 32°F (0°C) there is the risk of ice crystals forming in the sleeping animal's blood. This would be fatal. Like other hibernating mammals, dormice usually allow their body temperature to fluctuate with that of their surroundings. But if the temperature drops to within a fraction of a degree of freezing point, the animal's bodily functions "cut in," either making the animal wake up and move around, or keeping its temperature ticking over at just above freezing.

Dormice, like other hibernating mammals, must raise their body temperature to about 86°F (30°C) in order to wake up fully. They have special tissues in the shoulder region called brown fat. The sole

Young golden hamsters (Mesocricetus auratus) *leave home by thirty to forty days old* (right).

MATING

When the male and female meet for the first time, they sniff each other, first on the nose, then the flank gland, and lastly in the anal region.

FORAGING

The young are now ready to begin foraging for food without their mother's help.

Jane Burton/Bruce Coleman Ltd.

GROWING UP
The life of a young hamster

NEST BUILDING

The common hamster builds its nest from grasses, wool, and feathers in the burrow. Burrows vary in size and number of chambers.

BABIES

Between four and twelve young hamsters are born, hairless and blind.

MATURITY

The young leave home by thirty to forty days and are ready to mate by the following spring.

FROM BIRTH TO DEATH

COMMON HAMSTER
GESTATION: 18–20 DAYS
LITTER SIZE: 4–12
WEIGHT AT BIRTH: 0.2 OZ (5.7 G)
EYES OPEN: 12–14 DAYS
WEANING: 21 DAYS
INDEPENDENCE: 21–27 DAYS
SEXUAL MATURITY: 45–60 DAYS
LONGEVITY IN WILD: 2 YEARS

GOLDEN HAMSTER
GESTATION: ABOUT 16 DAYS
LITTER SIZE: 5–7
WEIGHT AT BIRTH: 0.07 OZ (2 G)
EYES OPEN: 12–14 DAYS
WEANING: 21–27 DAYS
SEXUAL MATURITY: 45–60 DAYS
LONGEVITY: 2–2.5 YEARS

COMMON DORMOUSE
GESTATION: 22–24 DAYS
LITTER SIZE: 2–7
EYES OPEN: 14–18 DAYS
WEANING: 21 DAYS
INDEPENDENCE: 40 DAYS
SEXUAL MATURITY: ABOUT ONE YEAR
LONGEVITY IN WILD: 4 YEARS (6 YEARS IN CAPTIVITY)

FAT DORMOUSE
GESTATION: 19–30 DAYS
LITTER SIZE: 2–10
EYES OPEN: 12–14 DAYS
WEANING: 28 DAYS
INDEPENDENCE: 25–28 DAYS
SEXUAL MATURITY: AFTER FIRST HIBERNATION
LONGEVITY IN WILD: UP TO 5 YEARS (UP TO 9 YEARS IN CAPTIVITY)

purpose of brown fat is to generate warmth when required. Exactly what triggers this is not known, but it is widely believed that when the outside temperature rises to a certain level, the brown fat begins to generate heat. When sufficient heat is generated, the sleeping dormouse's muscles start to shiver, generating even more heat. It may take about half an hour for a hibernating dormouse to wake up.

When the outside temperature rises, dormice wake from their hibernation. If this is just a warm patch in the winter, the dormouse may feed on the stored nuts before resuming its sleep. But this is a particularly perilous time for dormice. If they are awake for too long, they will use up their reserves of fat and may not have enough stored food to keep them going, and will starve to death. ■

931

STAUNCH SURVIVOR

MOST SPECIES OF HAMSTER AND DORMOUSE LOOK SET TO
SURVIVE IN SPITE OF HUMAN DISRUPTION TO THEIR HABITAT.
MANY, HOWEVER, HAVE BECOME INCREASINGLY RARE

The continued survival of most species of hamsters and dormice is not under any great threat. Indeed, initially, as the spread of agriculture began to widen—with people clearing and planting previously uncultivated land—many rodent species benefited. Cultivated crops brought with them a plentiful supply of food, seeds in particular, reducing the need to search far and wide. Well-fed animals will always breed more successfully than those fighting for survival in the face of starvation.

The result of this was that in some areas these animals began to be considered pests and, even now, large numbers are still trapped and killed

> OVER THE YEARS THE STATUS OF THE COMMON HAMSTER HAS CHANGED FROM COMMON PEST TO INCREASINGLY RARE IN SOME PARTS OF ITS RANGE

every year. However, because, by and large, they are able to produce considerable numbers of offspring annually, this culling does not pose a direct threat to most species.

A species of hamster that came to be regarded as a pest as a result of farming was one of the ratlike hamsters found in northeastern China—*Cricetulus triton*. After the penetration of this area by the Chinese Eastern Railway in the 19th century, enabling forests to be cleared for agriculture, this hamster began to invade new areas, stripping the newly cultivated corn of its grain. Nor did its destruction stop there; so fierce is this species of hamster that it attacked and killed other small rodents, including another species of hamster that had hitherto populated the area. In spite of this,

however, it is thought that it was looked upon favorably by the poor peasants of the countryside, who were able to dig up its hidden grain stores and use them to supplement their frugal existence.

HARDY AND ADAPTABLE

Hamsters are highly adaptable animals, capable of living in extremely inhospitable places, including

Tackling a meal larger than itself, a dormouse nibbles away at a fallen apple (right).

P. Morris

The edible dormouse can cause significant damage through feeding, as seen on this cherry tree.

THEN & NOW

The map below shows how the range of the common hamster is contracting.

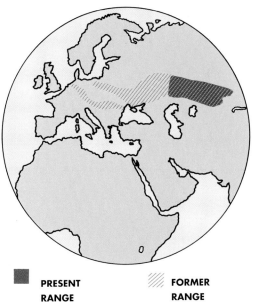

PRESENT RANGE **FORMER RANGE**

● In the past, the common hamster was considered a serious pest to agriculture, feeding as it does on a wide variety of seeds and cereals. Its burrowing habits also allowed it to nibble away at the roots of cultivated plants. The result of this was that it was widely trapped, until modern agricultural practices began to deprive it of its habitat.

● Still treated as a pest in parts of the southeast areas of its range, it has declined drastically in some western regions. In France and Belgium it is considered an endangered species, which means it is in danger of actual extinction. In Germany and the Netherlands it is listed as rare.

semiarid areas and deserts. Although man has spread further into these regions in many places, large tracts of them still remain untouched by human civilization, so hamsters in such areas are usually left undisturbed.

As we have seen, conflict usually occurs when rodents spread into areas cultivated for arable farming. Common hamsters, *Cricetus cricetus*, for example, can be serious agricultural pests in many parts of their range because of their habit of gathering and storing large quantities of food. This inevitably causes considerable damage to cultivated crops, corn in particular. In addition, the common hamster is also extremely partial to soybeans, potatoes, carrots, and sugar beets, all of which are important cash crops for humans.

DANGERS AND THREATS

However, modern technology seems to be getting its own back and in some parts of its range the number of common hamsters is beginning to decline. One of the main reasons for this is deep

> OVER THE CENTURIES, AGRICULTURE HAS CAUSED MANY RODENT POPULATIONS TO RISE BEFORE A DRAMATIC FALL

plowing. Mechanical plowing digs to a deeper depth than traditional plowing, thereby destroying the burrows of many hamsters. Also, modern farming methods make a farm a far less comfortable habitat generally for a rodent than was once the case. Sophisticated machines leave little in the way of gleanings in stubble fields for rodents, and steel grain stores are infinitely harder to penetrate than the previously used hessian sacks.

In some places, common hamsters are still trapped for their fur, which is used as lining for coats and jackets. However, modern-day attitudes are beginning to question the acceptability of using

SECRET OF SUCCESS

It is often stated that the entire wild golden hamster population was previously thought extinct and that the capture of twelve youngsters and a large female was the only thing that prevented this creature's complete disappearance. In truth, the golden hamster came from a remote area of northern Syria called Aleppo. Few people ventured into this area and no extensive surveys were carried out by naturalists. However, it is true that that small group of individuals—all from one litter—gave rise to virtually all the captive populations in laboratories and homes around the world until the early 1970s. In 1971, naturalists captured a further thirteen golden hamsters in the wild. These were taken to the United States.

A clue to the success of the golden hamster is in its ability to produce large numbers of young. A single female can produce some 400 offspring in her lifetime.

ENDANGERED ENVIRONMENT

P. Morris

ANCIENT WOODLANDS

Ancient woodlands, with their great variety of species of trees and other plants, are becoming increasingly rare across Europe. Cities are expanding as the human population continues to increase. More people means an ever-increasing demand for more agricultural produce, and the means to transport these quickly and cheaply from one part of the country to another.

Ancient forests are threatened by this need for expansion as large areas are cleared to make way for more farmland or new highways. Many species of plants and animals rely on these ancient woodlands for their survival. Dormice often build their nests in hollow or dead trees. In some carefully managed forestry plantations, such trees are removed and new saplings planted. While this does guarantee the survival of the forest, it does not take into account the fact that large numbers of animals need older trees for their nests or for food.

WIDESPREAD DISEASE

The reduction of suitable nesting sites means that populations of dormice are put under increased stress. As the number of nest sites is reduced, all the animals face greater competition to find a place, and they are forced to live in crowded home ranges, making the threat of disease more likely.

PEST OR RARE SPECIES? THE DAMAGE THE EDIBLE DORMOUSE DOES TO FRUIT PRODUCTION HAS MADE IT UNPOPULAR IN MANY PLACES.

CONSERVATION MEASURES

After many years of ripping out woodland to clear land for development, the fact that timber is once again a valuable resource has encouraged many landowners to return to more traditional ways of managing woodland, such as coppicing (felling trees) (see page 937).

HAMSTERS AND DORMICE IN DANGER

THE CHART BELOW SHOWS HOW THE INTERNATIONAL UNION FOR THE CONSERVATION OF NATURE (IUCN), OR THE WORLD CONSERVATION UNION, CLASSIFIES THE STATUS OF THE HAMSTER AND DORMOUSE:

FAT DORMOUSE	**RARE**
	IN BELGIUM, SPAIN, ROMANIA
	VULNERABLE
	IN CZECHOSLOVAKIA, GERMANY, HUNGARY
COMMON HAMSTER	**RARE**
	IN GERMANY AND THE NETHERLANDS

VULNERABLE INDICATES THAT THE ANIMAL IS LIKELY TO MOVE INTO THE ENDANGERED CATEGORY IF THINGS CONTINUE AS THEY ARE. *RARE* INDICATES THE ANIMAL POPULATION IS NOT AT PRESENT ENDANGERED OR VULNERABLE BUT IS AT RISK OF BECOMING SO.

animal fur for clothing, and the trapping of these animals is undoubtedly on the decrease.

Most of the species of dormice are woodland or forest dwellers and it is the destruction of their habitat in many areas that is the biggest threat to their survival. Across their range, the fat dormouse, common dormouse, garden dormouse, forest dormouse, mouselike dormouse, and Japanese dormouse have all suffered from habitat destruction. Many are now considered rare and given legal protection across their ranges. The mouselike dormouse is said to be one of the top ten endangered rodents in Europe.

As the habitat of many of these dormice is being destroyed, they are forced to forage for food and nesting sites in other areas. This means that

> MOST SPECIES OF DORMOUSE HAVE DECLINED IN NUMBERS DUE TO DESTRUCTION OF THEIR HABITAT

their native range becomes fragmented and populations get isolated from one another. Fat, or edible, dormice, for example, have invaded orchards and vineyards in many areas, while the inaccurately named garden dormouse—also a forest dweller—has adapted to living in swampy areas and cultivated fields in parts of its range. Although not threatened with extinction, as populations become isolated, their future can hang in the balance.

The reason why such isolated populations are threatened is that with the march of human civilization, it becomes increasingly difficult for

ENDANGERED ENVIRONMENT

ALONGSIDE MAN

PET HAMSTERS

For many years, hamsters—particularly golden hamsters—have made popular pets, being easily tamed, clean, and attractive and also requiring little space. However, potential owners should bear in mind that they are solitary animals that are mainly active during the night. If two or more adult hamsters are kept together, their apparently gentle nature undergoes a rapid change and they become extremely vicious, fighting with one another. Because they are seen during the day, when they are sleepy, it is easy to think they are quite indolent animals. In fact, they are extremely active at night and busy themselves continuously.

Hans Reinhard/ Bruce Coleman Ltd.

individual animals to move to new areas without having to negotiate their way through built-up areas, roads, agricultural land, and other man-made hazards. All of these present the rodents with an immediate threat to survival.

REPLANTING

As the human population increases worldwide and demands for food, housing, and wood also increase, the homes of many woodland species are becoming threatened. Replanting forests helps some species,

Golden hamsters are popular pets. Here one exercises by running inside a wheel.

Fresh vegetables and fruit make up part of the diet of a pet hamster.

but for most dormice only ancient woodland is able to support a healthy population, unless, that is, special provisions are made by supplying nesting sites and foraging areas. It is only in very old woodland that the hollow trees, in which many dormice like to build their nests, can be found.

A further threat to the habitat of many species of dormice, especially in parts of central Europe, is the mass dying off of trees because of the action of acid rain (see next page).

The threat to dormice is not a new thing, however, and some species have not even been as lucky as those mentioned above. On the Balearic Islands, in the Mediterranean, two species of dormice—known as the Balearic dormice, one of which was as big as a hamster—became extinct some 4,000–5,000 years ago. Because they lived on islands they not only had a limited range, but there was also only a limited area over which they could spread. So when

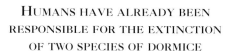

HUMANS HAVE ALREADY BEEN RESPONSIBLE FOR THE EXTINCTION OF TWO SPECIES OF DORMICE

humans began to colonize the islands the small rodents were easy prey for them and their domestic livestock—the absence of serious predators had made the dormice naturally unwary. Also, they could not compete for woodland that was quickly being turned into fields and grazing land. With nowhere else to go, in a comparatively short time these two species of dormice had vanished forever. ∎

Hans Reinhard/ Bruce Coleman Ltd.

INTO THE FUTURE

Despite its name, the common dormouse is almost as rare as any species of dormouse. Its numbers have declined throughout its range, mainly because of the decline, too, of traditional coppicing and the replacement of layered hazel hedgerows with fencing (see right). In the United Kingdom and parts of Europe, the common dormouse has disappeared from much of its former range. In England, for example, where it was once common throughout the country, it has disappeared from most midland and northern areas and is currently commonest in southwest England.

Fortunately, the common dormouse is now given legal protection in most countries where it is

PREDICTION

JAPANESE RARITY

The future of the Japanese dormouse, one of the rarest of all species of dormouse, will be assured by its listing in Japan's Cultural Properties Protection Act.

found, and the organization, English Nature, is trying to assure its future by working in conjunction with local conservation groups. A special license is granted enabling young dormice to be collected from certain nesting boxes during September and October. They have to be below a certain weight at which they would not survive hibernation—because

PREDICTION

DORMOUSE SUCCESS

More and more common dormice will be successfully reintroduced in the coming years thanks to breeding programs, such as the one run by English Nature.

there is insufficient fat to last them through the winter. They are kept indoors, fed constantly, and stopped from hibernating through that winter. As they grow, the dormice are moved to outside cages, where they also start to breed. The plan is to reintroduce them into areas where they have disappeared, especially protected woodland, where hazel coppicing is being practiced. ■

WOODLAND MANAGEMENT

Traditional management of broad-leaved woodland and hedgerows—that is coppicing and layering—ensured perfect habitats for the common dormouse, among others, for generations. Coppicing was the practice of felling trees but leaving a stump, from which new shoots would soon grow. In this way, woodland would constantly regenerate. In the same way, boundaries between fields were made by layering trees—hazel in particular—in such a way that they continued to grow.

Over the last fifty years or so, woodlands have been cleared by pulling out trees—roots and all—so that there is no chance of regrowth. Similarly, hedgerows have been ripped out and replaced by low-maintenance fencing. With the loss of the traditional practices the habitats of many dormouse species were also lost.

ACID RAIN DESTRUCTION

Acid rain is caused when pollutants, such as oxides of sulphur and nitrogen, are released into the atmosphere, usually by large industries burning fossil fuels. These pollutants dissolve in the water vapor in the air and are carried in the air currents. As it starts to rain, the pollutants are also released, poisoning the soil, trees, and rivers on which the rain falls. In some parts of the world, whole forests have been destroyed by acid rain, thereby destroying the habitat of many species of animal.

Illustration Steve Kingston

HARES

Leonard Lee Rue/Oxford Scientific Films

MAD MARCH HARES

THE SIGHT OF MADCAP HARES BOXING WILDLY IN A MEADOW REVEALS THEIR CLOWNISH SIDE—BUT FOR THE REST OF THE YEAR THEIR SENSES ARE TUNED TO PERFECTION IN A BID TO OUTWIT THEIR ENEMIES

The last snows have cleared from a meadow, but frost still lies in the shadowy depressions for several hours after sunrise. Crocuses have given way to primroses and daisies, following the timeless springtime pageant. Then, as if to shatter this reverie, a pair of hares rear up, exchange a few blows, then dash off. Others follow, then dart after each other joining one group and then another, standing bolt upright or falling down flat.

It is this sort of display that led to the expression "as mad as a March hare." Hares, normally cautious, solitary, and on the lookout for danger, let their guard down during their early springtime mating season. Their rituals appear haphazard and chaotic, and the hares seem oblivious to the threat posed by any predators in the vicinity. Closer study shows that some of the hares on the periphery are, in fact, acting as sentries—equally unusual behavior for these individualistic animals.

CLASSIFICATION

Hares and pikas are lagomorphs, members of an order that was long thought to be a subdivision of the rodents. Certain dental features show, however, that the two orders have always been distinct.

ORDER

Lagomorpha
(hares, rabbits, and pikas)

FAMILY

Ochotonidae
(pikas)

GENUS

Ochotona
(twenty-five species)

FAMILY

Leporidae
(rabbits and hares)

GENERA

Lepus
(hares and jackrabbits)

Bunolagus
(bushman hare)

Caprolagus
(hispid hare)

Nesolagus
(Sumatran hare)

The North American pika (below) is a lively and vocal species that lives among rocky outcrops.

Hares are herbivores, native or introduced to every continent except Antarctica. They favor open grassland habitats throughout this range, although some species live in forests, on sand dunes, or high up in mountains. Hares are solitary animals, spending the day in sheltered depressions called forms. This is an important difference between hares and their relatives, rabbits. Unlike rabbits, hares do not burrow. Many other features distinguish these two types of animal although the terms *hare* and *rabbit* are often used interchangeably in speech. Strictly speaking, only 23 species of the genus *Lepus* are "true" hares; the 24 species of the remaining ten leporid genera are rabbits. As a rule, hares are larger than rabbits.

FORM AND FUNCTION

The appearance of hares seems to bear out the principle that form follows function. Open terrain leaves them open to threats from predators, so their long ears act as an early warning system. Powerful hind legs, a light skeleton, and long-fibered muscles combine escape speed with high stamina.

Hares and rabbits form the family Leporidae (le-POR-id-ie) within the order Lagomorpha. The other lagomorph family, Ochotonidae (ok-o-TONE-id-ie), is

On the alert: Ears pricked and nose twitching, hares are blessed with superb senses.

Robert Maier/Aquila

INSIGHT

HARE OR RABBIT?

Hares differ from rabbits in a number of ways, some of which are not apparent to the casual observer. The most important difference is that hares are primarily "runners," while rabbits are mainly "burrowers." Anatomical features reflect this point. A hare's long legs and long-fibered muscles give it the stamina to outpace a pursuer over a long distance. The shorter legs and short-fibered muscles of a rabbit, on the other hand, are useful for quick sprints but are better used in building defensive burrows. Skeletal differences in the legs also give hares the edge in running.

Young hares are born above ground and can move about almost immediately. Rabbits, on the other hand, are born blind and hairless in the security of a burrow, and rely on their mother for protection. And finally, hares have 48 chromosomes whereas rabbits have only 44.

made up of twenty-five species of pika. These animals live mainly in mountainous regions of the northern hemisphere, although some species live on steppes, or in forests and deserts. The chunky pikas, with their short legs and squat bodies, do not really resemble hares and rabbits; at first glance they seem to be guinea pigs. Another difference is that pikas are active during the day. Some species have elaborate social structures, with families living together in large warrens. Others live most of their lives in pairs.

Pika habitats are usually remote. Most species live on talus—coarse, rocky debris—high in the mountains, retreating to cracks and crevices in the rocks at the first sign of danger. Despite their lack of stature, pikas can issue clear warning calls that can be heard up to 330 ft (100 m) away. This distinction has earned the pika a number of popular names, such as piping hare, calling hare, or whistling hare.

HARE DEVELOPMENT

Lagomorphs probably originated in northern Asia about 55 million years ago. The Leporidae family of hares and rabbits entered North America about 40 million years ago, where they underwent most of their development; more evolved forms recolonized Asia and Europe around seven million years ago. The Ochotonidae family of pikas developed in Asia about 30 million years ago. They spread into Africa, Europe, and North America about five million years ago. Since that time pikas have reduced their range until now they occupy only northeastern Asia and pockets of western North America, while hares have extended their range.

Both lagomorph families exhibited their adaptive changes early on in their evolutionary history. Hares, with their long ears, light skeletons, and powerful legs, are suited to habitats where they must forage widely and be able to escape rapidly. Pikas have nimble feet and a low center of gravity—essential in burrowing or scrambling along rough terrain. Their ears, which are shorter than those of hares, are still much longer than those of rodents of a similar size.

Having established these fundamental characteristics, lagomorphs have evolved slowly. There seem to be several reasons for this. Forest cover in many parts of the world gave way to open grasslands early on in the history of lagomorphs. This process suited hares, as it created vast swathes of open grassland. In effect the physical world was evolving to suit hares. Man-made clearances much later, reflecting the advance of cultivation, had a similarly beneficial effect on hare populations. Pikas benefited less from all these changes, and there is evidence of at least sixteen pika genera that became extinct. However, the early bodily adaptations remain appropriate for the rocky, mountainous habitats where most pikas live.

PARALLEL LINES

Hares are widespread in both the Old and New Worlds and demonstrate the broad adaptability of the genus to different habitats. The arctic hare thrives in the tundra of the northern regions of North America; its parallel is the mountain hare, which has adapted to similar terrain in northern Eurasia. The brown hare of Europe, Asia, and Africa lives on steppes, much like the white-tailed jackrabbit of North America. Desert habitats also feature similar hares: the Cape hare of arid regions of Africa, southwest Europe, and Asia and the black-tailed jackrabbit of the southwestern United States. ■

THE HARES' AND PIKAS' FAMILY TREE

Hares, rabbits, and pikas make up the order Lagomorpha. Zoologists generally agree that the pikas of Ochotona *comprise the only genus within the family Ochotonidae and that true hares make up a single genus—Lepus— of a family shared with rabbits, although popular and even early scientific nomenclature blurs the distinction between hares and rabbits.*

NORTHERN PIKA

Ochotona hyperborea
(ok-o-TOE-na hy-per-BO-ree-ya)

The northern or Siberian pika ranges across most of northeast Asia, with the Ural Mountains and Mongolia acting roughly as its western and southern boundaries. It thrives in mountain forests and in dry, rocky areas at the southern edge of its range.

AMERICAN PIKA

Ochotona princeps
(ok-o-TOE-na PRIN-seps)

The American pika has a wide range of isolated populations in western North America. It has adapted to many different habitats ranging in altitude from sea level to 10,000 ft (3,000 m). Like other pika species, it emits distinctive calls, which can identify individuals.

PINPOINTING PIKAS

Providing a universally agreed classification of all lagomorphs is almost impossible. One study might classify three different types of hare as subspecies of a single species; another might represent them as three different species. The taxonomy of pikas is especially difficult, partly because of the remoteness of their range. It has also been suggested that essential differences between proposed species are merely vocal—local populations on remote mountaintops might recognize others in their species purely through the call, rather than by visual examination. In this respect, studies of museum specimens might not be able to recognize the feature that distinguishes two or more species of similar appearance.

RABBIT

B/W illustration Ruth Grewcock. Color illustrations Angela Hargreaves/Wildlife Art Agency

BROWN HARE

Lepus europaeus
(LEP-us yoo-ro-PEE-us)

The brown, or European, hare is a large animal that is easily recognized by the tips of its ears, which have a large triangular patch of black on the back. Its native range extends across most of Europe except Ireland, Scandinavia, and the Iberian Peninsula.

OTHER *LEPUS* SPECIES:
JACKRABBITS (SIX SPECIES)
AFRICAN SAVANNA HARE
ARCTIC HARE
BURMESE HARE
CAPE HARE
CHINESE HARE
ETHIOPIAN HARE
INDIAN HARE
JAPANESE HARE
MANCHURIAN HARE
SAVANNA HARE
SCRUB HARE
SNOWSHOE HARE
WOOLLY HARE
YARKAND HARE

BUSHMAN RABBIT

Bunolagus monticularis
(boo-no-LAH-gus mon-tick-yoo-LAR-is)

The bushman hare is more properly known as the riverine rabbit, a clue to its riverside habitat. It is endangered, and exists only in scattered populations in the Cape Province of South Africa.

HISPID HARE
(OR BRISTLY RABBIT)

Caprolagus hispidus
(cap-ro-LAH-gus HIS-pid-us)

The hispid hare occurs in only a few pockets of its former range in the tall grasslands of northern India and southern Nepal. It shares its range with the Indian hare, although it is more usually classified as a rabbit.

SUMATRAN RABBIT

Nesolagus netscheri
(nez-o-LAH-gus NET-sher-ee)

The Sumatran rabbit is the rarest lagomorph, with only one confirmed sighting since 1916. Originally classified under the hare genus, Lepus, it was given its own genus in 1899. About the same size as a European rabbit, it is distinguished by its small ears and the dark stripes running down its back.

LAGOMORPHS

ANATOMY: THE BROWN HARE

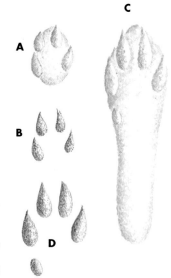

A

B

C

D

FOOTPRINTS

There are four digits on the hare's forefeet, as shown here on snow (A) and hard ground (B). The five-toed hind feet, also shown on snow (C) and hard ground (D), are much larger than the forefeet; they are up to 4.3 in (11 cm) long, giving the hare a strong base for powerful leaps. A hare's footprints are much deeper than a rabbit's.

MOVEMENT

A hare uses the same running pattern whether it is simply hopping (top) or making an escape run (above). In each case, the long hind legs move beyond the forelegs, enabling the hare to make a powerful leap. The tighter crouch when running gives the hare even more propulsion.

THE FUR

is long and soft, and even covers the feet. Some northern species molt to white during the winter.

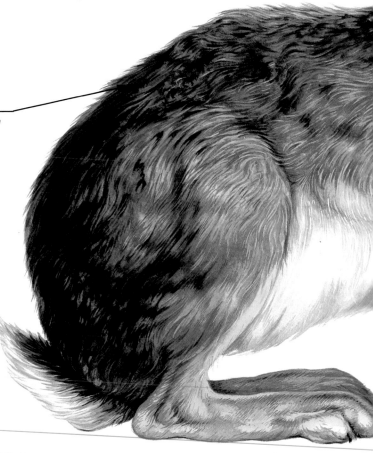

Lagomorphs range in size from the size of a small guinea pig to that of a large cat. The steppe pika (above right) is about 7 in (18 cm) long, while the brown hare (above left) measures 20–30 in (50–76 cm). The European rabbit (above center) has a head-body length of 10–11.5 in (25–29 cm).

X-RAY

HARE SKELETON

The skeletons of pikas and hares are suited to different habitats. The hare (right), with its more lithe body and powerful legs, is built for speed on open ground. Its pelvic girdle is enlarged to deal with the force of the hind legs. Overall, the skeleton is light in order to aid running.

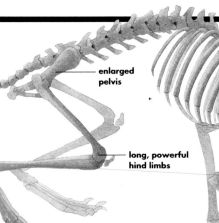

enlarged pelvis

long, powerful hind limbs

HARE'S HIND LEG

The hind limb of a hare is much longer than that of a rabbit, giving it extra running power. Both animals are digitigrade—that is, they walk "on tiptoe."

RABBIT'S HIND LEG

X-ray illustrations Elisabeth Smith

THE EARS

are very long, and the hare usually hears a threat before seeing it despite having a near-circular field of vision. The ears are laid flat along the head when the hare is feeding in the open or hiding from predators.

THE NOSE

has slitlike nostrils that can be opened and closed by a fold of skin above. The sense of smell is acute: Hares usually nest downwind from potential sources of danger. A Y-shaped naked groove extends from the nose down to the upper lip: This is the origin of the term harelip.

ANTELOPE JACKRABBIT

BLACK-TAILED JACKRABBIT

THE LEGS

are built for sustained speed over long distances, up to 50 mph (80 km/h). Hind legs are considerably longer than front legs and extend beyond the hare when it is hopping or running.

SNOWSHOE HARE

ARCTIC HARE

FACT FILE:

BROWN HARE

CLASSIFICATION

GENUS: *LEPUS*

SPECIES: *EUROPAEUS*

SIZE

HEAD–BODY LENGTH: 20–24 IN (51–61 CM)

TAIL LENGTH: 4 IN (10 CM)

SHOULDER HEIGHT: 12–16 IN (30–41 CM)

WEIGHT: 8.8–13.2 LB (4–6 KG)

WEIGHT AT BIRTH: 4.6 OZ (130 G)

COLORATION

BROWN OR GRAYISH-BROWN UPPER PARTS AND YELLOWISH CHEEKS AND UNDERPARTS

BLACK TIPS TO EARS

BLACK STRIPE ON UPPER SURFACE OF TAIL

FEATURES

ELONGATED EARS

ROUNDED BACK LEADING TO POWERFUL HIND LEGS

GENITALS OF MALES AND FEMALES LARGELY HIDDEN AND DIFFICULT TO DISTINGUISH

SHORT EXTERNAL TAIL OR "SCUT"

EAR LENGTH (LEFT)

The ears vary among hare species, although most are long and all have a black tip at the end. The ears of the desert-dwelling antelope jackrabbit are up to 20 cm (8 in) long: The animal can control its temperature by regulating blood flow through vessels in its ears.

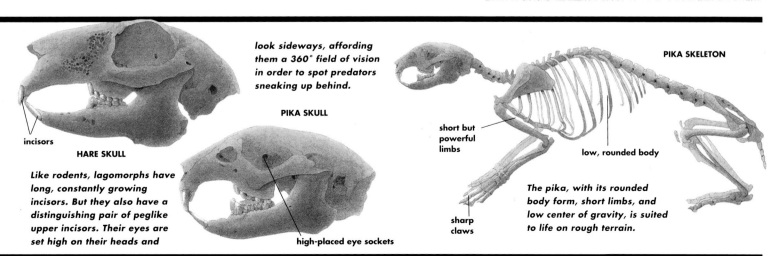

look sideways, affording them a 360° field of vision in order to spot predators sneaking up behind.

PIKA SKULL

PIKA SKELETON

incisors

HARE SKULL

Like rodents, lagomorphs have long, constantly growing incisors. But they also have a distinguishing pair of peglike upper incisors. Their eyes are set high on their heads and

high-placed eye sockets

short but powerful limbs

low, rounded body

sharp claws

The pika, with its rounded body form, short limbs, and low center of gravity, is suited to life on rough terrain.

Main illustration Rachel Lockwood/Wildlife Art Agency. Rabbit and hare heads Ruth Grewcock

Hop, Skip, and Jump

A HARE'S SAFETY LIES PARTLY IN ITS SPRINTER'S LIMBS AND TIRELESS STAMINA—BUT THOSE LONG EARS AND WIDE-ANGLE EYES ARE CRUCIAL EARLY WARNING SYSTEMS, AND SCENT ALSO PLAYS A VITAL ROLE

As a rule, hares are nocturnal. They spend the day in the form, rising at dusk to feed. The European brown hare eats its last meal at dawn before returning to its form to rest. Careful not to leave a set of tracks or scent, it crosses and recrosses its own path: This buys it time in case a predator follows the track. The form does not hide the hare, although the coat acts as good camouflage—so the hare must be ready for danger at a moment's notice. Lying down in its "nest," the hare can look around with a 360-degree field of vision; its acute senses of hearing and smell also serve it well in defense. Once assured that there is no danger, the hare falls into a state of semisleep, ears pressed flat to its crouching body.

ONE EYE OPEN

Hares rarely enter deep sleep: They may sleep for no more than a minute a day. Sensing danger, the hare crouches low and freezes; running away is a means of escape but might betray the location of the form if the hare bolts too soon. If it does run, the hare can sustain speeds of more than 43 mph (70 km/h). Its flight is not usually a headlong rush; most hares are familiar enough with their surroundings to make for another hiding place, and will use sudden twists and turns to throw off a pursuer. Hares swim well and are not afraid to dash into a watery refuge.

During the day a hare also grooms, by nibbling and licking the coat and ears and washing the face. A clean coat prevents heat loss; in fact, hares are often the smallest mammals in their habitats to survive winter without a den or burrow. Another aim of this cleaning is to spread secretions from glands near the nose, chin, and anus to the body and paws. The hare uses its own scent-markers to orient itself.

Late in the afternoon or sometimes nearer dusk, hares leave their forms to begin feeding. This is the one time—apart from breeding—when they gather in numbers. Groups of a dozen or more can be seen heading for rich feeding grounds, sometimes up to 9 mi (15 km) away. Having reached, for example, a field of alfalfa or winter corn, the group then disperses and the hares are on their own again.

Some hares behave differently. The arctic hare, for example, lives on the northern tundra. Though bleak and bare, this habitat still supports plenty of predators, such as wolves, foxes, and owls, although there is less cover for the hares. Arctic hares may flee from predators by hopping on their hind feet, like kangaroos, or moving together as a flock. Young hares form herds of about twenty, following the tracks of musk oxen in winter to graze on exposed plants or racing together for up to a mile (just less than two kilometers) to escape a wolf.

Pikas spend much of their lives sunbathing, stoking up plenty of body warmth (above).

Larry West/Frank Lane Picture Agency

John Shaw/NHPA

*in*SIGHT

WHITE WINTER COATS

A hare's constant vigilance and ability to make speedy escapes are evidence that the threat of predators is never far away. Some northern species even molt to produce a white winter coat as camouflage on open snowfields. The arctic hare, the most northerly dwelling of all hares, and the snowshoe hare of North America are good examples. Their outer layer of long hairs changes twice a year.

The summer coat is brown, but as autumn sets in, new white hairs begin to appear—and as they grow, the brown hairs fall out. The changing number of daylight hours triggers this change, and the coat is fully white by winter. Members of the same species living at the southern end of the range never grow a white coat. Other species that turn white in winter are the mountain hare, the Japanese hare, and the white-tailed jackrabbit.

The brown hare also molts, but the difference between summer and winter coats is usually one of thickness and length of the fur. However, the brownish fur serves as excellent camouflage during the summer, when many of the longer grasses have been eaten or have withered and dried to take on a soft brown color.

Pikas are built for a very different way of life. Most species live on loose, rocky habitats known as taluses, sheltering in crevices. A webbing of fur on the soles of their feet gives them purchase on smooth rock surfaces. A few species, living on steppes or in semiarid deserts, dig their own earth dens.

Resting by night, pikas spend their days feeding or gathering food; this is vital, since food is needed for the winter when the ground is snowbound. Pikas collect surplus food, drying it in a "haying" process, and then storing the haystacks for the winter. Like hares, pikas do not hibernate. In fact they have trouble with overheating. At 104°F (40°C) their normal body temperature is very high, so in summer they spend most of the day in near inactivity in order to keep cool. This internal heating system is so efficient that pikas will sometimes be observed sunning themselves on rocks when the ambient air temperature is only 0°F (–17°C)! ∎

The snowshoe hare's coat turns white in winter to match the North American landscape.

HABITATS

Almost all hares live in open countryside. Their powerful legs, light skeleton, and muscular system make them suited to a life of foraging over long distances and fleeing from predators. They occupy habitats ranging from agricultural pastureland and arctic tundra to tropical savanna and desert. They usually, however, rely on the presence of some form of cover, such as bushes or even rocks, for shelter.

The brown, or European, hare typifies this generalized portrait of hare habitats. It has a native range that covers most of Europe except Scandinavia, Ireland, and the Iberian Peninsula, and extends east into Russia, the Caucasus, and Turkey. This hare thrives on mixed farmland, where cover is provided by shrubs and hedges. Elsewhere, brown hares occupy moorland, salt marsh, open woodland, alpine grassland, and near-desert conditions.

DESERT AND FOREST

The black-tailed jackrabbit of the southwestern United States has an almost totally arid range. It will venture onto farmland in California, but can thrive among the sparse cover of sagebrush and mesquite-snakeweed in the Mojave Desert. Its sandy coat is well suited to the arid terrain. Several

Crouched in its form, a white-tailed jackrabbit keeps an eye open and alert to any signs of trouble.

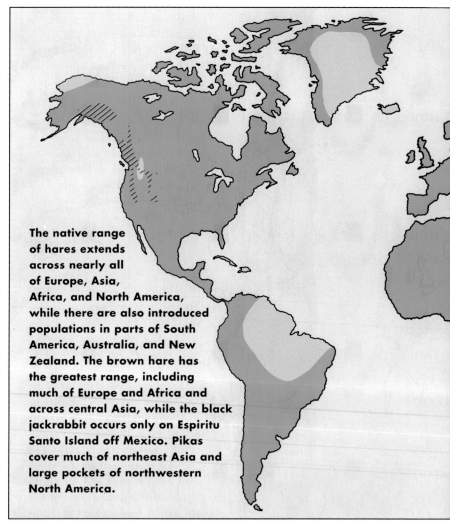

The native range of hares extends across nearly all of Europe, Asia, Africa, and North America, while there are also introduced populations in parts of South America, Australia, and New Zealand. The brown hare has the greatest range, including much of Europe and Africa and across central Asia, while the black jackrabbit occurs only on Espiritu Santo Island off Mexico. Pikas cover much of northeast Asia and large pockets of northwestern North America.

Rod Planck/NHPA

(in)SIGHT

MASS MIGRATION

Hares usually rely on their own defenses to warn them about predators, and they usually keep to a small range—with some tagged individuals never having strayed more than 2 mi (3 km) in their life.

Unusual circumstances can change this behavioral pattern dramatically. Brown hares, for example, will migrate if food supplies are hit by a sudden change in natural conditions. In 1928 a three-day blizzard in Ukraine sent a population of brown hares from the steppes into a nature preserve some 43 mi (70 km) away. On the night that the storm ended, observers saw thousands of hares bounding across the moonlit field. The next morning, however, marks in the snow revealed that the hares had carefully stepped in the leaders' tracks to avoid leaving too many telltale prints.

DISTRIBUTION

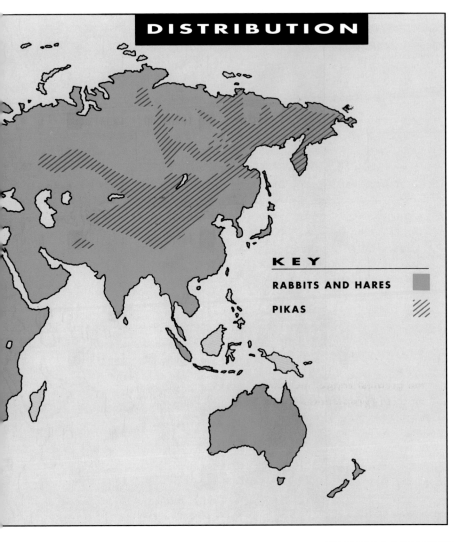

KEY

RABBITS AND HARES

PIKAS

species—the collared and American pikas—are typical rock-dwellers. These pikas live in climates that produce harsh winters, so haymaking is a crucial part of their daily routine from early autumn onward.

The steppe pika is a burrower that ranges from the Volga and Ural Mountains east to the Siberian-Chinese border. It prefers sites where the moist soil is covered with grasses and bushes. The steppe pika, like other burrowing pikas, is more social than the rock-dwellers, and lives in family groups.

Lagomorphs are important elements in the food chains and overall ecology throughout their range, and hares of upland regions perform an unusual service to their habitat. They descend to forage among the richer vegetation on the valley floor, and usually defecate on their journeys to or from their forms, which are sometimes several hundred yards (meters) higher up the valley slopes. These fertile deposits reverse the more common downhill flow of nutrients in an ecosystem, enabling plants to colonize upward. Hares in the dry African scrubland also contribute to plant mobility, although less systematically. Plant seeds and burrs often get snagged on their fur, only to fall and germinate some distance away.

PIKAS AS PREY

Pikas, too, are vital to the ecosystem. They play the role of middle-sized generalist plant-eater in the food web, and, as such, they are an important prey base for predatory birds and mammals. This importance increases in the winter, when most rodents of comparative size hibernate.

hare species go against "normal" hare instinct by shunning open ground in favor of forest cover. Two species of Manchurian hare live in mixed coniferous and deciduous forest, with dense curtains of vines and creepers. The Cape hare has one of the widest natural ranges of any hare, inhabiting almost every landscape that can support hares. Its range encompasses large areas of Africa, across the Middle East into much of central Asia. Within this range it is found on the rich equatorial grasslands of Africa, nearly 8,202 ft (2,500 m) up in alpine meadows or on the cold, rocky floor of the Gobi Desert in Mongolia.

In contrast to hares, pikas are linked to just two main habitats. Most live on rock-strewn uplands known as taluses, provided by the mountain ranges of central and northern Asia and western North America. The other pikas—a minority overall—den in burrows on steppes or in forests or shrubland. The alpine pika and northern pika of central and northern Asia, and the two North American pika

A dryland specialist, the savanna hare lives in Kenya, Sudan, southern Africa, and the Sahara.

Populations of steppe-dwelling pika species sometimes reach peaks, at which time the pikas become the primary food source of a wide variety of predators. Alpine and northern pikas are the principal food sources of weasels and sables, while stone martens, booted eagles, and levantine vipers rely on Afghan pikas as their primary prey. Even larger predators such as wolves and brown bears sometimes depend on pikas: The stomach of one brown bear contained twenty-five pikas!

Burrowing pikas often share their burrows with other mammals and birds. Afghan pikas coexist with jirds (burrowing rodents), gerbils, hamsters, and shrews. The finches and jays of the Tibetan plateau favor the burrows of the black-lipped pika as nesting habitats. These burrowing pikas also contribute to the ecosystem by recycling soil. Like other digging animals, they aid in the formation, mixing, and aeration of soil. This process also improves the infiltration of water into soil. In fact such burrowing acts as a defense against soil erosion, which is often caused by overgrazing by domestic livestock. This work on the soil also benefits the local flora by increasing the diversity and productivity of plants. Excrement and leftover stores enrich the soil, leading to increased concentrations of nitrogen, calcium, and phosphorous.

T. Kitchen & V. Hurst/NHPA

FOCUS ON

THE YUKON TERRITORY

The Yukon Territory in northwest Canada is a land of craggy mountains, dense forest, and open tundra, and contains Canada's highest peak, Mt. Logan (19,524 ft/5,951 m). This wilderness area is about twice the size of the state of New York, although fewer than 30,000 people live there.

Despite the severity of the weather, the Yukon supports a wide range of plant and animal life. Wild flowers, herbs, and grasses flourish in the brief summer, and conifers provide nourishment for many animal species even when 7 ft (2.1 m) of snow cover the ground. Wolves, coyotes, bears, hawks, and eagles prey on ground-dwelling vertebrates or on the trout and salmon in the rivers and lakes.

Collared pikas and snowshoe hares are key players in this ecosystem, constantly aware of the threat from predators but adept at finding sustenance from a range of vegetation. Each has adapted to survive the harsh winters. The snowshoe hare, as its name implies, uses its broad feet to tread lightly across deep snow to find food sources in the forest. The collared pika literally "makes hay while the sun shines," storing up winter supplies of food among the rocks and crevices of its upland habitat.

TEMPERATURE AND RAINFALL

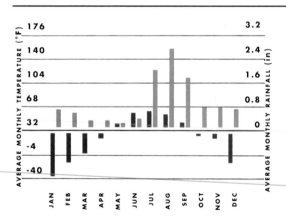

■ TEMPERATURE

■ RAINFALL

The Yukon has a continental climate. The long winter is bitterly cold, but the brief summer can be warm, and with summer rainfall also reaching a peak, a surprisingly large range of seasonal plants is supported.

Pikas in rocky habitats can help plants to sprout on previously "barren" sites: The remains of their hay piles can lead directly to plant colonization. Moreover, nitrogen-rich pika droppings nourish the plant life. Certain species of the mustard family, for example, grow only on the burrows of Pallas's pikas in the Gobi Desert. Set against these benefits, however, are the negative effects of widespread foraging over the delicate soil surface. Pikas often reduce the number of flowering alpine plants and destabilize plant cover by their habit of eating small trees. ■

NEIGHBORS

The Yukon's wild and remote mountains, lakes, and valleys are a haven for wildlife. Here, the pikas and hares run the gauntlet of some of North America's biggest and deadliest predators.

GOLDEN EAGLE

The golden eagle soars aloft scanning the ground for prey, before diving with sharp talons outstretched.

AMERICAN MARTEN

An agile climber, the marten spends most of its time in trees where it preys on squirrels.

Neighbor and enemy illustrations Kim Thompson, except: eagle by Edwina Goldstone/Wildlife Art Agency; coyote by Evi Antoniou

THE YUKON

The Yukon Territory has a narrow coastline on the Beaufort Sea, but a narrow strip of its western neighbor, Alaska, separates its southwest corner from the Pacific. Much of the Yukon lies in or between parallel mountain ranges—the Alaska and Rockies in the west and the Mackenzie in the east.

Beaufort Sea

Yukon R.

ALASKA

YUKON

Pacific Ocean

ENEMIES

COYOTE
Like its Old World cousins, the jackals, the coyote is an adept survivor that includes almost any prey in its diet.

WOLF
A skilled pack hunter, the wolf will not miss an opportunity to snap up a pika caught out in the open.

WOLVERINE

The wolverine lives on the ground, but can climb trees in pursuit of other animals or simply to gather berries.

MULE DEER

The mule deer moves seasonally between sheltered valleys and higher meadows.

PACIFIC SALMON

Young Pacific salmon live in the ocean but return to breed in rivers and lakes when they are mature.

SNOW GOOSE

This goose ranges widely in arctic and subarctic regions, breeding on open tundra or on lake islands.

BROWN (GRIZZLY) BEAR

The grizzly is one of the world's largest carnivores, although its diet includes berries and plant matter.

FOOD AND FEEDING

Because they do not hibernate, hares and pikas must be able to feed all year round, even in conditions of extreme cold and snow cover. Their normal diet is usually available only in spring and summer, in the form of grass, clovers, ferns, and sedges. For many species of hare and pika, the winter diet is dictated by necessity, and alters to include woody matter, such as twigs, bark, and buds.

The double digestion system of hares is vital to their survival. In spring they glean nutrients, such as proteins and amino acids, from grasses and herbs. But plants respond to the drier summer period by storing these nitrogen-rich substances in their roots and rhizomes. The withered stems become much less nutritionally rich for the hares, which do not dig for food. Instead by digesting and then redigesting the vegetation, they derive sufficient nutrients.

When feeding, the hare remains close to the ground, with its ears laid flat along its back. Hares will feed on or along cultivated fields, but studies of stomach contents show that more than half of the contents are noncrop vegetation. In this respect hares retain a taste for the food of their original habitat, the steppes. Brown hares can spend the day at

Manfred Danegger/NHPA

The brown hare can be most agile when food is the prize. Here (left), *an adult reaches up to browse on willow leaves and twigs—a rich source of nutrients when grasses cannot easily be found.*

in SIGHT

DOUBLE DIGESTION

Hares and pikas, like rabbits, have a digestive technique that allows them to derive the maximum nourishment from their food. They excrete two types of pellet: a hard, spherical pellet (true feces) and another that is soft and covered in mucus, known as a cecotroph (SEE-ko-trof).

The small intestine of a lagomorph is actually quite long, and its twisted shape provides a great deal of surface area for digesting food and absorbing nutrients. The cecum, located at the junction with the large intestine, contains digestive bacteria. Cecotrophs form in the cecum during the initial digestion and absorb vitamin B_1.

The animal eats the cecotrophs at once, sometimes directly from the anus and before they reach the ground. They are then digested a second time in a part of the stomach called the cardiac zone. This reingestion of vitamin-rich pellets serves much the same purpose as cud-chewing among ruminants such as cattle.

Illustrations Peter David Scott/Wildlife Art Agency

MAKING HAY

Unlike the hare, the pika simply does not have the option of changing to other fresh food sources to see it through the lean months. So it busies itself in harvesting "hay"— grass stems and herbs that it reaps (right), *dries, and carefully stacks.*

THORNY FARE

For any animal that does not hibernate in winter, finding enough food on the iron-hard, snowbound ground is a daily struggle. At this time, hares turn to trees, shrubs, and even brambles (left).

some distance from their grazing spots—distances of up to just over a mile (1.8 km) are common—and a nocturnal feeding session can involve 9 mi (14.5 km) of traveling.

Unlike hares, pikas are active during the day but their high body temperature restricts their movements during the warmest hours. They usually feed at sunrise and in the late afternoon. Rock-dwelling species search for food along the edge of the talus; burrowers can often find food nearer their nests. Pikas eat a wide range of plants, including the leaves, flowers, and stalks of grasses, sedges, mosses, lichens, and twigs off shrubs. Unlike rodents they cannot grasp plants with their forepaws; instead they eat from the cut end downward.

GIANT HAYSTACKS

Pikas prepare for winter snow cover by gathering food stores from late summer onward. Some rock-dwelling species store these piles under rocks or in crevices, but most pikas dry them out in the sun and then build "haystacks" in the open or among shrubs. These haystacks can become quite large, sometimes reaching 13 lb (5.9 kg). Moreover, the Mongolian pika carries stones measuring up to 2 in (5 cm) in its mouth to protect its piles of hay from the wind. These piles can be temptations for other animals living nearby. Voles, shrews, and even reindeer head for pika territories to feed off the stored hay. ■

TERRITORY

Hares are generally unsociable creatures, and individuals mark and maintain a territory to guard food sources against others. Scent markers within a territory also help a hare acquaint itself with, and remember, potential escape routes. Urine and fecal pellets provide part of the scent "trail," but hares also use pungent glandular secretions. Some of these glands lie on the head—a pin-sized gland at the tip of the nose, and others on the chin. The hare often rubs its nose against twigs to leave its signature smell. The elaborate cleaning rituals observed help spread these secretions from the head to the paws and other parts of the body. There are other glands near the anus, and a hare leaves yet more scent "calling cards" each time it sits on its haunches.

Although hares have keen hearing, they lack any repertoire of calls, apart from a plaintive wail when caught by a predator. The black ear tips declare a hare's presence in an area, and many hares have a territorial display—raising the tail high—to show the white underside to others.

Habitat plays a large part in the size and definition of hare territory, and two North American species illustrate this point. The snowshoe hare is the most widespread of all New World hares, ranging from Alaska to

Harvesting time (right): The adults of some pika species will share a territory, pooling such assets as sheltering niches, nesting sites, and key food sources.

STACKING UP

Each North American pika defends its own territory, and needs to keep watch over its precious haystacks (below); there are plenty of thieving neighbors who will stoop to burglary to boost their own winter supplies.

Newfoundland and as far south as Tennessee and New Mexico. It is one of the few hare species to favor forest cover, and individual territories reflect the richness of the forest vegetation: In thick cover these can be as small as 15 acres (6 hectares).

Arctic hares, on the other hand, inhabit a hostile tundra landscape, and they are among the few species to form herds. During the winter, when food is most scarce, arctic hares move from one location to another in search of food. Such a group will have a "territory" of up to 13.5 sq mi (35 sq km).

PIKA TERRITORIES
Because of their more remote habitats, the social interactions of pikas are something of a mystery to observers. Males of most pika species are thought to establish individual territories, and the pika's ability

ⓘⓝSIGHT

CALLS OF THE WILD

Unlike hares and rabbits, pikas have a rich vocabulary of calls—loud, distinct, and varied. These calls can be heard as far away as 1.2 mi (2 km); the pika makes the call by "throwing its voice," using much the same technique as a ventriloquist.

The calls can be grouped generally into two categories: long and short. The long call is made up of a chattering sound followed by a series of loud, sharp whistles. These calls, which can be traced to individuals, are given by males during the breeding season.

Short calls are usually one- or two-note squeaks; they are used by both sexes in a variety of circumstances. Sometimes the pika will perch on a prominent outcrop and issue such a call as if to announce its presence in a territory or to acknowledge a similar call from another pika. The short call is also used when pikas are chasing or being chased by other pikas. Most significantly, the call is also used as a danger signal, warning other pikas about the presence of predators.

Dieter & Mary Plage/Survival Anglia

to call—unique among lagomorphs—probably plays a part in establishing these territories during the breeding season. Recent studies of American pikas have shed new light on territoriality and social organization. Each adult is territorial, with little difference in the size of male and female territories. There is an average population density of six to ten animals per 2.5 acres (1 hectare). Adjacent home ranges are held by individuals of the opposite sex. Moreover, territories are "inherited" by members of the same sex, maintaining the male-female balance.

The northern pika, an Asian rock-dwelling species, is also strictly territorial. Male and female adults live in a joint territory, with individuals remaining in this fixed area for life. The northern pika marks this territory by rubbing its neck gland

ROCK SINGER

The pika's short call (below) is a terse squeak with many uses; its most vital role lies in warning others of approaching danger.

on stones or by leaving urine deposits. Males and females use a short call to communicate within a territory. Curiously, these male-female territorial partnerships are not based on a breeding strategy. During the breeding season, males travel up to 660 ft (201 m) to visit three other females; at the same time females are visited by several males. Steppe-dwelling pikas live in higher population densities. Burrows become the home of family units, comprising an adult male, an adult female, several juveniles, and a number of smaller pikas.

Pika territories, maintained during the spring and summer, take on an added significance in the winter. The essential hay piles, so carefully gathered, become the target of theft—not just by other mammal species but also by neighboring pikas! ■

Illustration Chris Shields/Wildlife Art Agency

COURTSHIP

The breeding season is the one period when hares seem to throw caution to the wind, as they gather in large numbers in open fields. Tolerance of fellow hares evaporates as males box with each other—and with females. Their pungent secretions, which play an important part in the breeding rituals, also act as a tip-off to predators.

Despite the well-known behavior of "mad March hares," the breeding season actually begins at around the shortest day of the year (at the end of December), and it is not uncommon for females to be pregnant in January. During this winter period adult hares undergo physiological changes that prepare them for the imminent reproductive season. Taking their cue from the amount of daylight, the testes of a male increase in size and the female's ovaries also enlarge.

These internal changes are reflected in differences in the way the hares behave. They begin to prefer more open and exposed spaces, and large groups may be observed during the daylight hours on snowy fields. These large congregations allow hares the chance to choose suitable partners, and the presence of many other hares seems to induce a type of "mob psychology" uncharacteristic of such a normally solitary animal.

The breeding activity that follows, when studied more closely, does prove to be full of rituals and

in SIGHT

ON DIFFERENT SCENTS

Hares and pikas have secretory glands that enable them to send out signals to others of the same species. Yet curiously, these secretions can be used in opposite ways during courtship.

Hares—both male and female—use scent to attract members of the opposite sex during the breeding season. The male hare's overriding aim in laying down this odorous trail is attraction—even if the scent also attracts other males or even predators. Other males can always be dealt with through boxing or chasing off.

Pikas, living in territories with more limited food sources, have a less combative courtship. Aggressive behavior between males is avoided, and the trails of scent are used specifically to discourage unwelcome visits by neighboring males.

Illustration Robin Boutell/Wildlife Art Agency

TAKE THAT!
Surprisingly, fisticuffs usually occur between a male and female (right), *rather than between two rival males. The physicality of the courtship is vital in that it incites the female to ovulate.*

Leaping lagomorphs! Spring is in the air and in the hare's step (right) as its thoughts turn to courtship and breeding. Kick-boxing helps chase off rival suitors that get in the way.

Sylvestris Fotoservice/NHPA

to cuddle and fondle her partner and then warding him off with blows of her forepaws. Males, not realizing that the female is not ready for copulation—which must be tied to ovulation—often rain down blows on the females.

Near the end of the courtship the pair spend a few days in a "pairing run," in which displays of coyness or frustration wind down. The pair then stop, enabling the male to rub the female's abdomen; she accepts these advances and may even push herself across the male's back. This action induces ovulation, which signals the time to copulate.

SEVERAL MALE HARES MAY SOMETIMES BE SEEN CHASING A SINGLE RECEPTIVE FEMALE DURING THE BREEDING SEASON

Copulation itself lasts only about ten seconds, although neither male nor female see this as an anticlimax. The female remains standing and raises the rear of her body to allow the male to mount her. She finishes with a "copulation leap," extending her hind legs outward and throwing off the male.

Most hare species follow this breeding pattern, although there are a few minor differences. The snowshoe hare, which lives in forests and avoids open spaces even for feeding, indulges in similar paired chases in the courtship period. Females sometimes lead a curious courtship parade, followed by several males thumping the ground as they go. Mountain hares have similar parades, with males following a female at a distance of 7–65 ft (2.1–20 m).

LONERS

Breeding among most pikas is very different, completely lacking the frenzied aggression and headlong dashes of mating hares. In some respects monogamy—a single pairing—is imposed on pikas, due largely to their isolated home ranges and also because of the difficulty of a single male defending more than one female against other intruding males.

The choice of a mate is linked to territory for many pika species. Typically a male enlarges his territory in the spring to share the territory of a neighboring female. This pairing continues through the breeding season, but the female begins to reassert territorial independence by late summer or early autumn. By the time "haying" is complete, the territories are separate again. Burrowing pikas have more complicated mating arrangements—males may have two female mates or vice versa. Again, territory plays a crucial role: The death of a male or female leads to the takeover of a mate or mates by a neighbor. ∎

stylized patterns of routine. Hares begin to make initial social contacts at this agreed mating place. Certain stimuli, such as glandular scent and visual flashes of the tail or dark ear tips cause a large number of males and females to form a "group courtship," usually in the late morning or early afternoon. This grouping helps widen the pool of potential partners and also provides safety in numbers.

BOXING MATCHES

The courtship itself is often protracted, with males and females pairing off, usually initiated by the male's pursuit of the female. Dominant males will chase smaller, inferior males from any female who is, or is about to be, sexually receptive, and therefore get more chances to mate than the subordinate males. The male's frenzied chase after his intended mate is punctuated with quieter periods of rest and feeding, and occasionally with the well-known boxing matches. Throughout much of this time the female displays coyness toward the male, seeming

LIFE CYCLE

Despite the wide range of climate and terrain encompassed by the various species of hare, breeding patterns point to some underlying consistency. As a rule, females in most species produce about ten young each year. However, the strategies used to achieve this total differ greatly—usually in relation to latitude. Northern species tend to have one large litter annually, with up to eight young being born. At the other extreme are the species living nearer the equator, where females have up to eight litters of only one or two young during the year.

This level of consistency contrasts with the pattern of many rabbit species. Cottontails in a selected area, for example, produce anywhere between ten and thirty-five young in a year. Snowshoe hares are the nearest equivalent to rabbits in this respect, with reproductive output varying between areas and years from about six to eighteen annually.

MATING

(above) *reaches its peak in March and results in a glut of infants in early summer, although some hares in southerly climates may breed throughout the year.*

YOUNG HARES

(left) *leave the natal area soon after weaning; many are lost to foxes or diseases.*

Pikas also exhibit different breeding strategies, but these differences tend to reflect variations in habitat. Rock inhabitants usually have two litters— each with fewer than five offspring—annually. Few of the second litter survive. Den-dwelling pikas give birth to more offspring in the course of the year, and females reach sexual maturity early, so that some born in spring will reproduce in the summer of the same year. The difference is explained by the shorter summers at higher altitudes, which reduces the time available to raise young, as well as the shortage of food compared with the fertile prairies. Significantly, however, the talus-dwellers have longer life spans—up to seven years—and their populations remain stable over time.

Pikas are born blind and helpless but grow rapidly on their mother's rich milk.

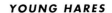

Dieter & Mary Plage/Survival Anglia

GROWING UP
The life of a young brown hare

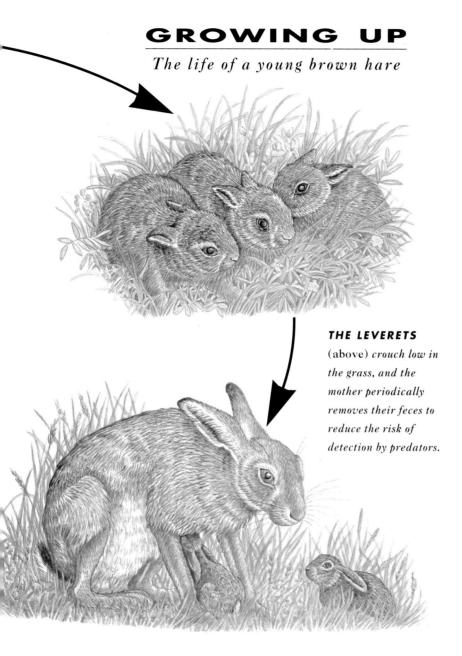

THE LEVERETS
(above) *crouch low in the grass, and the mother periodically removes their feces to reduce the risk of detection by predators.*

SUCKLING

lasts only a month or so; the mother sits up to offer her teats to the tiny young (above). *The leverets are utterly helpless and clueless at this stage; they have been known to follow birds about in the hope of a feed.*

The March breeding antics of most hares leads to a "baby boom" in May and June. Females give birth to a litter of up to four leverets (young hares); there might be as many as three more litters in the same year. Desert-dwelling species, such as the antelope jackrabbit of the southwest, tend to have smaller litters, and litter size depends on rainfall.

The actual birth and development of the young provides a major difference with rabbits. The leverets are born in the open, they are well furred at birth, their eyes are open, and they can move about soon after birth.

Each leveret soon makes its own form, but joins others to be visited by their mother for twilight nursing. This is one of the few times that hares use vocal contact: The mother warns the leverets of her approach with a low call; their responses help her locate them. Nursing itself lasts only ten minutes. Such a brief time is possible because hare's milk, with its high fat and protein content, is much richer than that of goats or cows.

During this four-week nursing period the leverets grow from a birth weight of about 4.6 oz (130 g) to about 2.2 lb (1 kg). For about a week before weaning they will have been supplementing the milk diet with plant material. The leverets must fend for themselves after being weaned, although it takes about another five to six months before they attain full adult weight. As a rule young hares do not breed in their first year—the late-born leverets would stand little chance of surviving the winter.

EFFICIENT MOTHERS

Pikas are born in litters ranging in size from one to thirteen. Newborn pikas are blind and totally helpless, but they grow quickly on a diet of the mother's rich milk, doubling their 0.2 oz (6 g) birth weight within about five days. Maternal care among pikas is very limited. The Gansu pika, a burrowing species native to central China, is a typical example: Mothers sometimes spend as little as ten minutes nursing their young. Males play no part at all in the care of these young. Young pikas continue suckling until they are about three weeks old; they must disperse several days later.

Representatives of some pika species, such as the American pika, have territories that have been held by a male or female for many generations. The likelihood of a juvenile—of either sex—reaching adulthood depends on its ability to find a vacant territory. The problem is made more acute by the inhospitable terrain that adjoins most talus areas: juveniles crossing these exposed zones are easily dispatched by predators. The result, in many talus-dwelling pika communities, is a type of genetic stagnation, and periodic inbreeding is common. ■

FROM BIRTH TO DEATH

STEPPE PIKA	BROWN HARE
GESTATION: 20–24 DAYS	**GESTATION:** 42–44 DAYS
LITTER SIZE: 7–13	**LITTER SIZE:** 2–4
BREEDING: TWICE YEARLY (SPRING AND SUMMER)	**BREEDING:** FEBRUARY–OCTOBER
WEIGHT AT BIRTH: 0.2 oz (6–7 G)	**WEIGHT AT BIRTH:** 4.6 oz (130 G)
EYES OPEN: 8–9 DAYS	**EYES OPEN:** AT BIRTH
WEANING: 3 WEEKS	**WEANING:** 30 DAYS
FORAGING: 30 DAYS	**FORAGING:** 3 WEEKS
SEXUAL MATURITY: 25–30 DAYS IN THE FEMALE; PROBABLY 6–8 WEEKS IN THE MALE	**SEXUAL MATURITY:** 1 YEAR
LONGEVITY: 4 YEARS	**LONGEVITY:** USUALLY 4 YEARS IN WILD (A MAXIMUM 12.5 YEARS RECORDED)

Illustrations Carol Roberts

959

BOUNCING BACK

ALTHOUGH THEY LACK THE AMAZING BREEDING CAPACITY OF RABBITS, MOST HARES AND PIKAS CAN STILL SUSTAIN THEIR POPULATIONS IN THE FACE OF PERSECUTION AND HABITAT ALTERATION BY HUMANKIND

H ares and pikas do not face any overall threat to survival, although some individual species with restricted habitats have become rare. Generally, hares are protected by their rapid breeding rate and adaptability to a wide range of open habitats. As a genus *Lepus* seems to be extending its range.

Pikas, on the other hand, are "past their peak" in evolutionary terms, having been reduced to a single genus from a one-time high-point of about seventeen. However, remaining populations of pikas are at the fringes of, or far removed from, major centers of human population. That fact stands in their favor in terms of longer-term survival.

SPORT HUNTING

Hares were one of the first animals to be hunted widely and they remain the principal game animal in many areas. Hunting methods include shooting, snaring, and netting. The snowshoe hare has been a traditional mainstay of Canadian Indians, trappers, and settlers. Hordes of these and other hare species are killed each year: Polish hunters dispatch up to 700,000 brown hares each year; their Japanese counterparts kill some 800,000 Japanese hares annually.

Most of these figures relate to sport hunting; up until the 1930s, however, hares and pikas were trapped so their pelts could be used to make felt. Market forces came to the rescue of these lagomorphs. Hunters in pre-Revolutionary Russia regularly sold more than six million skins of hares each year. This business continued to be an important revenue-earner for the Soviet government. Since the 1930s, however, the price fetched for these skins has not risen. Even the Soviet authorities recognized the free-market message, and the numbers killed trailed off considerably. Elsewhere in Europe the message was the same: The number of hare skins on the market was halved in the decade of 1955–1965, and the downward trend continues. The market for pika furs, which also make high-quality felt, has also stagnated.

Habitat alteration has a deep impact on hares, particularly among species with a restricted range. The Hainan hare, native to the island of Hainan off China, normally favors the dry grasslands of the island but has had its range drastically reduced by the introduction of new, intensive agricultural methods. Previously the hare could actually thrive on traditionally farmed land, where scrub and plantain provided cover and food. Widespread agricultural clearances, along with hunting, have put intense pressure on hare populations all over the island.

Stephen Krasseman/NHPA

In spite of how cuddly it is, the pika (above) *is a major agricultural pest in some countries.*

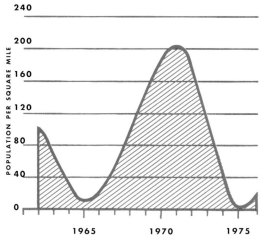

Jeff Lepore/Photo Researchers/Oxford Scientific Films

This graph shows a typical population cycle of the snowshoe hare in central Alberta, Canada.

POPULATION PER SQUARE MILE

240

200

160

120

80

40

0

1965   1970   1975

SNOWSHOE FORTUNES

The snowshoe hare is the smallest *Lepus* species and is also the most widespread hare in North America. Overall populations follow fixed cycles, with peak densities up to 300 times higher than the valleys. A complete population cycle lasts 8–11 years, usually averaging 10 years.

Peak population densities—about 75 per acre (30 per hectare)—have a profound impact on local vegetation. Aspen and willow trees, favorite winter sources of food, become badly ringed by the hares. The resulting scarcity of food is often cited as the trigger of a population decline, with predators also controlling numbers. These population cycles are believed to occur over a large geographical range.

Other hare species thrive in the presence of habitat changes. Cape and Abyssinian hares occupy a range of East African habitats that includes open grassland, savanna, steppe, and semidesert conditions. Both species have added to this range by encroaching on pasture that has been overgrazed by domestic livestock. The black-tailed jackrabbit, occupying similar terrains in the southwestern United States and Mexico, also benefits from such overgrazing.

This adaptability could prove to be a two-edged sword, however. New irrigation techniques and the introduction of green crops to former desert areas

The snowshoe hare has traditionally been a source of meat and fur for native North Americans.

undoubtedly attracts hares. There are increasing reports of damage to forestry, agriculture, and groundnut crops in India and Pakistan. The damage has been attributed to the Indian hare. Demands by farmers for controlling these hares could lead to extermination in wider areas.

PESTS

Some pika species are seen as pests; the Afghan pika is a particular thorn in the side of Asian farmers. These pikas eat crops, such as wheat and potatoes, but the farmers are most concerned about damage caused during the winter; when green plants are scarce, the pikas turn to apple and walnut trees. Stripping a ring of bark 10–16 in (25–41 cm) above the ground, these pikas can kill about 5 percent and damage nearly half of the trees in a severe winter. Black-lipped and Daurian pikas are also blamed for agricultural damage in Asia, and Pallas's pika may be a focus for plague. This combination of farming and public health concerns has put pressure on governments to adopt strict control measures.

ALONGSIDE MAN

SCIENTIFIC STUDY

Hares and rabbits have long been used in laboratory research, but scientific advances have been overshadowed by the dubious morality of the use of lagomorphs in cosmetic testing, and by some publicized cancer tests. Animal rights groups often target labs where lagomorphs are used in experiments.

Pikas are sometimes described as resembling guinea pigs. That analogy has become even more appropriate as scientists recognize their usefulness as laboratory animals. They are easy to feed, maintain, and clean, and do not need much space.

Field studies of pikas are also shedding new light in many scientific fields, notably genetics. The isolated habitats and inherited territories of many talus-dwelling species have led to many generations of inbreeding. In effect these pikas are "textbook cases" of small population biology. Newly developed techniques of inquiry, with sympathetic methods of experimentation, should lead to conclusions with profound importance for lagomorphs, mammals, and even human medicine.

M. Callan/Frank Lane Picture Agency

The measures used to control populations are still evolving, with authorities still searching for a method of population control that is not ecologically disruptive. One poison used to control Pallas's pikas in the 1970s, known as sevin, has been abandoned after it proved to sterilize animals and affect whole ecosystems. Compound 1080, a pika-controlling chemical, was abandoned in 1978 when it was found to kill the carnivores that ate pikas!

KIND KILLING

Recent North American research on lagomorph control has emphasized holistic and systems-based approaches. There, the focus was on damage to

The mountain hare is not officially hunted for sport, but falls into conflict with British gamekeepers because it feeds occasionally on heather, an important food source for grouse on the northern moors.

forestry and agriculture caused by snowshoe hares and jackrabbits. Nonlethal methods, seen as the ideal, included the use of repellents that mimicked the scents of skunks, minks, or even predators. Other "kinder" means of control included fencing, using plastic tubing around individual seedlings, and adjusting the density of trees in a particular stand.

The studies also examined lethal methods of lagomorph control, with a view to cost and environmental concerns. Shooting and trapping were seen as time-consuming, expensive, and cruel. One of the least disruptive toxic baiting methods employed anticoagulents. These work by delaying the clotting of blood, causing death by hemorrhaging.

These conclusions are laudable, but they are notably cost-intensive. Anticoagulants, for example, are expensive and must be distributed in large quantities in order to be effective. The Chinese already employ anticoagulants in their control measures, but the high cost has confined these programs to cities and major agricultural areas.

International studies of lagomorph populations show that five genera require complete protection. Their populations are so small, and their habitats so restricted, that they are severely endangered. In each case, the genus comprises only a single species. None of these genera, strictly speaking, is a true representative of either hares or pikas, although three of these animals—the hispid hare, bushman hare, and Sumatran hare—have at one time been grouped with hares. The Tehuantepec jackrabbit (a true hare) as well as the Kozlov's and Muli pikas, face similar threats. ■

INTO THE FUTURE

Hares and pikas stand to benefit from increased scientific studies of community dynamics, research that places them in the context of the wildlife around them. Already organizations such as the Lagomorph Specialist Group (see right) are compiling data on all known species, focusing on their roles in local ecosystems and food chains.

These studies have already alerted the scientific community about endangered species. Equally importantly, they have far-reaching consequences on activities that bring humans and lagomorphs into close contact. These activities include agriculture, hunting, forestry, and development generally.

Such interspecific study is not new. Records of the Hudson Bay Company in Canada going back to the 18th century reflect the population cycles of the snowshoe hare and their effect on other animals in the locality. Fur trappers knew that the increased

PREDICTION

SURVIVAL OVER A WIDE RANGE
Intensive farming techniques featuring the use of weed killers will check the population of the European brown hare and some American jackrabbits, but overall these and other wide-ranging species should hold their own. Hares and pikas with very restricted ranges will continue to be threatened by habitat alteration.

hare population in turn supports greater numbers of predators such as lynxes, foxes, and martens.

Classification is another area of urgency. Some naturalists see this as the first step in building an "action plan" to protect hares and pikas. Shortages of—and sometimes the inappropriateness of—museum specimens has led to great variations in the taxonomy of hares and pikas. Even naming has become a source of confusion. Reputable zoologists agree that there are 19–23 "true" hares within the genus *Lepus*; however, they use up to 30 specific names to describe them. Likewise, one pika has been treated as a single species by one author and included in three separate species in other pika classifications.

It seems important, when in doubt, to err on the side of caution by according full species status to certain populations. Without that recognition and focus for conservation, species whose identity is in doubt might become extinct before the world recognizes their uniqueness. ∎

THE SPECIALISTS

The International Union for the Conservation of Nature and the Species Survival Commission established the Lagomorph Specialist Group (LSG) in 1978. Since then the LSG has been studying lagomorphs, attracting biologists from all over the world. The LSG has helped publicize the key role played by lagomorphs in ecosystems worldwide. It has also singled out species and habitats for monitoring and protection; in doing so it has called for a clearer, more comprehensive study of lagomorph classification. Despite constant financial constraints, this group—and others like it—contribute greatly to the work of the IUCN. Its studies support reports to CITES—the Convention on International Trade in Endangered Species of Wild Fauna and Flora.

HARE POPULATIONS

A number of hare species have been introduced to parts of the world in which they do not occur naturally. These transplants have greatly enlarged the range of the hares as well as boosting their populations.

Hare populations are not as explosive as those of rabbits, so many of these introductions have not harmed the new hare habitat. For example the brown or European hare has been successfully introduced to Australia and New Zealand, Argentina and Chile, as well as into a small pocket of southeastern Canada and the northeastern United States. Likewise, the mountain hare has been successfully integrated into the Faeroes, the Scottish Isles, and parts of northern England. The black-tailed jackrabbit, normally a native of the arid southwest of the United States, thrives in new habitats along the eastern coast of the United States.

Some transplants, however, have disrupted the local ecosystem. Following the introduction of the snowshoe hare on Newfoundland in the 1860s, the native arctic hare was restricted to the western highlands of the island.

Illustration Joanne Cowne

HEDGEHOGS

RELATIONS

Hedgehogs and tenrecs belong to the order Insectivora, or insect-eating mammals. Other members of this order include:

SHREWS

MOLES

GOLDEN MOLES

DESMANS

SOLENODONS

Geoff du Feu/Planet Earth Pictures

Hedgehogs and tenrecs are members of the insectivore order. This order, which contains over 300 species of small animals that feed mainly on insects and other invertebrates, can be divided into three suborders. Hedgehogs and moonrats belong to one suborder; tenrecs to another.

ORDER

Insectivora
(insect-eating mammals)

HEDGEHOG SUBORDER

Erinaceomorpha

FAMILY

Erinaceidae

TWO SUBFAMILIES

NINE GENERA

TWENTY SPECIES

TENREC SUBORDER

Tenrecormorpha

FAMILY

Tenrecidae

THREE SUBFAMILIES

TEN GENERA

TWENTY-THREE SPECIES

DEFENDERS OF THE EARTH

TRUNDLING ALONG A GRASSY VERGE OR ROLLED UP IN A DEFENSIVE SPINY BALL, THE HEDGEHOG IS A POPULAR CREATURE IN EUROPE. LESS WELL KNOWN ARE ITS RELATIVES ON THE AFRICAN ISLAND OF MADAGASCAR, THE TENRECS

In recent years the hedgehog has become a welcome sight in many towns and cities in Europe, where it is often adopted as a free-ranging pet. Its placid nature, cute appearance, and shambling walk have won over many who would have once regarded it as a flea-ridden nuisance.

The hedgehog's most distinctive feature is, of course, its thick, spiny coat, which covers the upper part of its relatively short and bulky body. Each spine is equivalent to a group of hairs fused together. These do not cover the whole of the body: The belly, tail, legs, and face are clothed instead with sparse, coarse, gray-brown hair. When a hedgehog is threatened, it rolls into a ball to protect its vulnerable fleshy parts, an ability made possible by a flexible, muscular spine and a loose cover of skin.

The hedgehog is a primitive creature that appears much as it did when it first appeared some 15 million years ago. The teeth, feet, and skeleton

The common tenrec (above) *and the European hedgehog*
(right) *shared a common evolutionary heritage prior to the
geological split of Madagascar from the African mainland.*

are all very basic, and the small brain is simple in
structure. Even so, for all its simplicity, this has
been a remarkably successful design. In the
hedgehog's long evolutionary life span, it has
persisted in more or less unchanged form for
longer than most living mammals.

Hedgehogs belong to the mammalian order
called the insectivores, within which they form a
distinctive family called the Erinaceidae, which
consists of about twenty species. Most of these look
much the same as the familiar European hedgehog;

ALTHOUGH THEY BELONG TO THE HEDGE-
HOG FAMILY, MOONRATS OR GYMNURES
DO NOT SHARE THE DISTINCTIVE SPINES

the exceptions are the moonrats or gymnures (JIM-
nyures), which live in the forests of Southeast Asia
and China and have hair instead of spines. These
are the least studied of all hedgehogs. Most of them
have the appearance of large shrews, alert and agile
with elongated snouts and soft fur, but the greater
moonrat is about the same size as a rabbit and is
covered in coarse black hair.

The typical spiny hedgehogs are divided into
four groups: Eurasian hedgehogs, African
hedgehogs, desert hedgehogs, and long-eared
hedgehogs. All four are distinguished by the
presence of a big toe, or hallux, on their hind foot,
their facial coloring, and the size of the spineless

966

MODERN PRIMITIVES

Insectivores are in the mammalian order that consists of such creatures as shrews, moles, and the rare solenodons of the Caribbean. They are generally considered to resemble the original stock from which all other mammals—including humans—are derived. Over time, many insectivores have developed their own particular characteristics, such as the hedgehog's spines, which are not found in their ancient ancestors.

They do, however, share such characteristics as a small, relatively undeveloped brain, simple dentition, internal testes, a flat-footed (plantigrade) gait, and a cloaca (klo-A-ka)—a common genital, urinary, and fecal passage.

parting that extends from the back of the forehead, exposing a naked scalp.

The evolutionary history of the hedgehog is poorly known because they, like their ancestors, are forest-dwelling creatures. When animals die in the forest, their remains are likely to be eaten or dispersed. They are rarely buried in mud or preserved in a way that results in fossils being available for scientists to study. Most of what is known about the insectivores' evolutionary history

Masahiro Iijima/Ardea

Looking very similar to a shrew, an albino greater moonrat uses its long snout to forage for food.

967

is based on interpretations of a few teeth and bones.

Over 10 million years ago, another group of ancient insectivores, the tenrecs, arrived in Madagascar, the island off the southeast coast of Africa. Here they discovered a promised land: As one of the first mammalian groups to arrive on the island, they did not have to compete with an established fauna. So while most of their ancestors on the African mainland perished in the face of competition from other insectivores, the tenrecs were able to evolve a variety of forms to exploit all the different types of available habitat.

THE TENRECS, UNHINDERED BY PREDATORS, EVOLVED A GREAT DIVERSITY OF BODY FORMS

As a result, tenrecs look like otters, shrews, moles, and, of course, hedgehogs—they are the most diverse of all the living insectivores.

It seems likely that the tenrecs are even more ancient than the hedgehogs but, as the fossil record is so scanty, it is hard to know what their ancestors looked like. Many of the insectivore fossils discovered so far are giant-sized creatures, evolutionary experiments that simply didn't work. ■

(A)NCESTORS

The shrewlike megazostrodon (meg-a-ZOSS-tro-don, *bottom*) lived in the dinosaur-dominated world of 220 million years ago and was among the very first mammals to evolve. Only 5 in (12 cm) in length, it had a skeleton very similar to today's hedgehogs.

Deinogalerix (day-no-GAL-a-rix, *top*) lived about 15 million years ago in southern Italy, which was then a group of islands. Isolated from predators or competitors, it grew to the size of a modern-day terrier, hunting small mammals, birds, and reptiles.

THE HEDGEHOG'S FAMILY TREE

This family tree shows the relationships between the different members of the insectivore order. This order is divided into six families containing about 350 different species among them. The diagram shows that the closest relation to the hedgehog and tenrec is the giant golden mole. All the insectivores are descended from a common ancestor, though each species has gradually evolved its own specialized features—the hedgehog's spines, for example.

COMMON TENREC
Tenrec ecaudatus (TEN-rek ek-o-DAY-tus)

There are about thirty-three very diverse species of tenrec. The majority of these are found only on the island of Madagascar. The exceptions are the otter shrews, aquatic creatures found in West and Central Africa.

GIANT GOLDEN MOLE

INSECTIVORES

EUROPEAN HEDGEHOG
Erinaceus europaeus (erin-a-SEE-us yoo-ro-PAY-us)

The Erinaceidae family is divided into two subfamilies: the Erinaceinae or hedgehogs, which includes the well-known and widely distributed European hedgehog, and the Echinosoricinae—the much less familiar moonrats or gymnures (sometimes called spineless hedgehogs) of Southeast Asia. Altogether there are twenty different species of Erinaceidae.

OTHER SPECIES IN THIS FAMILY INCLUDE:
DESERT HEDGEHOG
LONG-EARED HEDGEHOG
GREATER AND LESSER MOONRATS

SOLENODONS

DESMAN

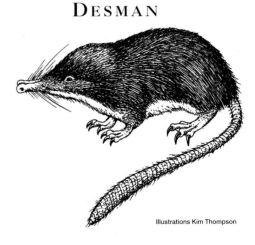

EUROPEAN COMMON SHREW

Illustrations Kim Thompson

ANATOMY:
THE HEDGEHOG

HEDGEHOG **TENREC**

THE LONG SPINES

cover only the hedgehog's back. Its face, throat, chest, belly, and legs are covered with a coarse, long fur.

The European species is among the largest of hedgehogs, reaching up to 9 in (22.9 cm) in length and weighing about 2 lb (0.91 kg). The common tenrec is the largest living insectivore, measuring about 15 in (38 cm) long.

THE LONG NOSE

helps the hedgehog to detect prey. Hedgehog noses are constantly damp, and this moisture enhances their sense of smell.

HIND FOOT

FOREFOOT

There is a marked difference between the footprints of the forefeet and hind feet (above)—it's easy to mistake them for the prints of two different creatures. The feet have powerful claws for digging (below)— most hedgehogs have five claws, the one exception being the four-toed or white-bellied hedgehog.

Illustrations Barry Croucher/Wildlife Art Agency

X

R A Y

Compared to other mammals, the hedgehog's skeleton is unspecialized. The main difference lies in the shortness of the neck. This may make it easier for the hedgehog to roll itself up into a spiky ball at the first sign of danger by contracting special muscles in its skin. The animal can remain in this position for hours, if necessary.

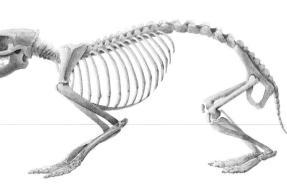
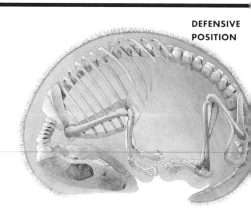

DEFENSIVE POSITION

X-ray illustrations Elisabeth Smith

CROSS SECTION THROUGH SKIN

Each spine has its narrowest section—or "neck"—just above the point at which it ends, in a bulb shape, buried in the skin (right). If the hedgehog falls or is hit by something, the spine necks bend and thus absorb the force of the blow.

neck of spine

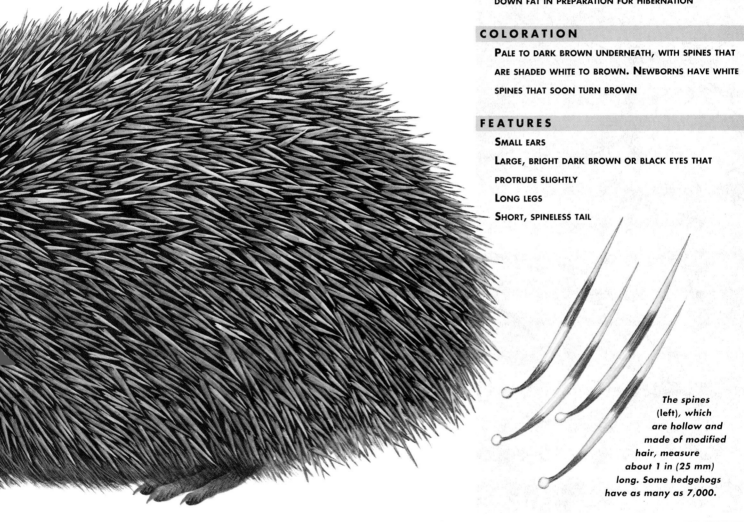

FACT FILE:
THE EUROPEAN HEDGEHOG

CLASSIFICATION

GENUS: *ERINACEOUS*

SPECIES: *EUROPAEUS*

SIZE

HEAD–BODY LENGTH: 9 IN (22.9 CM)

WEIGHT: 3 LB (1.4 KG)

TAIL LENGTH: 0.75 IN (2 CM)

SPINE LENGTH: 1 IN (2–3 CM)

WEIGHT AT BIRTH: 1 OZ (28 G)

A HEDGEHOG MAY DOUBLE ITS WEIGHT AS IT LAYS DOWN FAT IN PREPARATION FOR HIBERNATION

COLORATION

PALE TO DARK BROWN UNDERNEATH, WITH SPINES THAT ARE SHADED WHITE TO BROWN. NEWBORNS HAVE WHITE SPINES THAT SOON TURN BROWN

FEATURES

SMALL EARS

LARGE, BRIGHT DARK BROWN OR BLACK EYES THAT PROTRUDE SLIGHTLY

LONG LEGS

SHORT, SPINELESS TAIL

The spines (left), which are hollow and made of modified hair, measure about 1 in (25 mm) long. Some hedgehogs have as many as 7,000.

Viewed from the front, it is easy to see the hedgehog's large front teeth. Though they look like canines, they are, in fact, specialized incisors; the small canines lie behind them. Adult hedgehogs have thirty-six sharply pointed teeth.

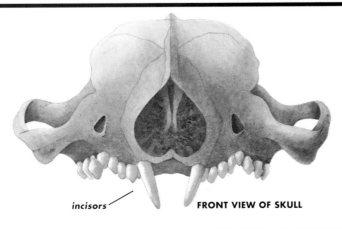

incisors

FRONT VIEW OF SKULL

SIDE VIEW OF SKULL

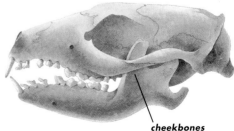

cheekbones

Hedgehogs, like other insectivores, have elongated, flattened skulls with small braincases. Unlike the shrews and moles, though, hedgehogs have fully formed cheekbones.

MIDNIGHT RAMBLERS

AS THE EVENING DRAWS NEAR, THESE SECRETIVE FORAGERS LEAVE THE WARMTH OF THEIR LEAFY NESTS AND SET OUT ON THEIR NIGHTTIME TRAVELS IN SEARCH OF FOOD

Hedgehogs and tenrecs are generally nocturnal creatures that spend their waking hours pottering about, hunting for the earthworms, insects, and beetles on which they feed. Their lives are usually fairly uncomplicated, with little sign of social or territorial behavior, though scent seems to play an important role in communication.

Greater and lesser moonrats in captivity will use secretions from their anal glands to scent mark their territory, while hedgehogs leave a scent trail behind them as they walk. This may contain information about the sex of the animal—male hedgehogs have been observed changing the direction of their travels to follow the scent of a female.

> **HEDGEHOGS LEAD UNCOMPLICATED LIVES, SPENDING MOST OF THEIR TIME LOOKING FOR THE SMALL ANIMALS ON WHICH THEY FEED**

Unlike the shy and retiring moonrats, hedgehogs are able to venture out into areas where there is no natural cover because they have a thick coat of sharp spines and are well protected against predators. When an enemy approaches, a hedgehog will erect its spines and freeze, but, if touched, it will quickly curl into a ball with its head and feet tucked in. The result is an impenetrable spiky ball.

Some species of tenrec also adopt this defense. The small streaked tenrecs have a number of barbed, detachable spines on their neck and, by bucking their head, they can drive these into any would-be predators. If the common tenrec is provoked, it will advance, gaping, hissing, and head-bucking. It can also deliver a very nasty bite—a large male has a 4-inch (10-centimeter) gape, 0.6-inch (1.5-centimeter) canines, and huge jaw muscles.

With these very effective defenses against predators, hedgehogs and tenrecs do not need to be strictly nocturnal to escape danger and may sometimes be seen foraging in daylight hours. Yet it is more productive for them to hunt at night as most of the small invertebrate animals they feed on are, for their own reasons, nocturnal.

NIGHTTIME FOOD

Some of these prey animals avoid daytime warmth and sunshine, others seek to prevent water loss by evaporation, and many benefit from moist, dew-laden night air. Most of them come out in the dark to avoid being seen and eaten. So, essentially, hedgehogs are nocturnal because most of their food is, too.

Hedgehogs and most tenrecs are solitary animals, except when females are rearing their

This African hedgehog (above) *has got the better of a lizard, while a Eurasian hedgehog confronted by an adder* (right) *raises its spines in self-defense.*

Hedgehogs usually walk with an unhurried, shambling gait, though they can run quickly and are fairly good swimmers (below).

Spichtinger/ZEFA

young. An exception are the streaked tenrecs, which live in family groups of as many as eighteen animals of up to three related generations. Members of the group may forage all together, in smaller subgroups, or alone. When they forage together they keep in contact by stridulating, or rubbing the stiff quills on their back together to make a clicking noise. This is especially important to help keep the mother and young together in dense cover at night.

HEDGEHOG BRAINPOWER
Though normally considered unathletic creatures, hedgehogs can run faster than a man can walk. They can also swim and, contrary to popular belief, climb readily. They have been known to hibernate in thatched roofs and climb into upstairs bedrooms, and garden fences appear to present few obstacles.

Hedgehogs lead simple lives and do not have powers of reasoning to solve complex problems. However, in captivity they have been taught very easy tasks such as choosing between a black and white trap door, if food is placed behind one but not the other. Similarly, they have learned to distinguish between shapes and symbols, but only to a limited extent. Some hedgehogs will also learn to come when their name is called.

INDIVIDUAL BEHAVIOR
Hedgehogs are individually very variable in behavior and personality. In captivity it is noticeable that some hedgehogs are tame from the start, while others never even uncurl without signs of acute anxiety. Some captive hedgehogs are similar to dogs and cats in that they will behave in a relaxed way with their normal keeper, but never settle down with anyone else. Even hedgehogs in the same litter grow up with different personalities. ■

HABITATS

Hedgehogs occupy a wide variety of habitats and can be found in the forests, plains, and deserts of Europe, Asia, and Africa. One species also occurs in New Zealand, introduced there by settlers in the last century, though there are no hedgehogs in Australia or the Americas.

THE EUROPEAN HEDGEHOG HAS ADAPTED WELL TO THE CHANGING LANDSCAPE AND IS ONE OF THE FEW MAMMALS TO THRIVE IN AN URBAN ENVIRONMENT

Some species, such as long-eared and desert hedgehogs, have adapted to the hot and arid regions of Asia and North Africa. Others, such as the species found in western Europe, were originally animals of the deciduous woodland, and are scarce or absent in areas of mountain, moorland, and marsh.

WELL ADAPTED

Although much of Europe's deciduous woodland has been lost to cultivation, the European hedgehog has adapted well to the changing landscape and now frequents farmland and hedgerows. It is one of the few mammals that seem to thrive in urban habitats, inhabiting parks and gardens, even ones deep in the heart of cities.

Unlike many mammals, hedgehogs are also found in Ireland and on many of the offshore islands of Britain and Europe, though few of these can have

DISTRIBUTION

The European hedgehog inhabits woodland, grassland, and hedgerows throughout the British Isles and most of Europe, into Russia, around the Black Sea, in eastern China, and in New Zealand, while the Algerian hedgehog is found along the hot, dry Mediterranean coast of North Africa. The African species are found throughout much of Africa and the Middle East into Afghanistan and Pakistan and the long-eared hedgehog in desert and scrub throughout the Near and Middle East, southwestern Asia, across Russia, Mongolia, and China. Tenrecs can be found in Madagascar.

KEY

- EUROPEAN HEDGEHOG
- ALGERIAN HEDGEHOG
- AFRICAN HEDGEHOGS
- TENRECS
- LONG-EARED HEDGEHOG

Ashod Francis Papazian/NHPA

been colonized naturally. It is much more likely that they found their way there by accident, scooped up with loads of thatching, peat, or animal fodder—though in some cases the animals were introduced deliberately to islands.

EXPANDED HABITAT

The territory of the closely related eastern hedgehog overlaps with its western European neighbor's along a rough line drawn from the Baltic to the Adriatic. Its range then extends into the steppes and forested plains of the east. In recent times it, too, has expanded its habitat to include cultivated land, villages, and towns.

In contrast to the wide distribution of hedgehogs, all the thirty-two species of tenrecs come from

This long-eared hedgehog lives in Syria and, to protect itself from the heat in summer, digs a burrow to provide a cool daytime resting place.

Madagascar alone, although the common tenrec has also been introduced to other islands in the Indian Ocean. Tenrecs occupy widely divergent habitats including both evergreen and deciduous forests, streams, rivers, and lakes.

HEDGEHOGS LIVING IN COOLER CLIMATES NEED NOT ONLY A WARM, SAFE PLACE FOR HIBERNATION, BUT A COOL NEST TO REST IN DURING HOT SUMMER DAYS

The aquatic tenrecs like fast-flowing freshwater streams and rivers, and are often closely associated with the iris plant. The rice tenrecs also tend to be found near water, particularly rice paddies (hence their name), freshwater streams, and large lakes. Most of the long-tailed tenrecs are confined to moist, forested areas. The common tenrec can tolerate a variety of habitats, both moist and dry, while the

lesser hedgehog tenrec is adapted to the dry southwest of Madagascar. Streaked tenrecs live in the moist lowland forests of eastern Madagascar.

Hedgehogs often build nests in hedgerows, clumps of vegetation, or piles of leaves where they rest during the day. Secluded places that provide shelter and warmth, such as dense vegetation, are vital in cooler climates because hedgehogs must hibernate in order to survive the winter cold.

COPING WITH THE CLIMATE
Elaborate nests are less important during the summer months, though females construct a large "nursery nest" for their families. If the weather is warm, hedgehogs may just rest in suitably thick vegetation or under a bush and not bother to build

The European hedgehog (above) has a variable gestation period, which may be because of the unpredictable weather: A cold spring could lead to a food shortage and thus to the slower development of the embryo.

ZEFA

KEY FACTS

● Long-eared and desert hedgehogs must avoid the heat of the day; they use their powerful legs and claws to dig burrows 16–20 in (41–51 cm) deep for a cool, moist resting place.

● Male hedgehogs, with their larger home ranges, travel farther and faster than females, sometimes as far as 2 miles (3 km) a night.

● The shrew hedgehog lives in cool, damp Far-Eastern forests at altitudes of over 6,560 ft (2,000 m).

a nest at all. So a good supply of leaves from deciduous trees is essential for survival in winter. Where there are no broad leaves there are rarely hedgehogs—so it is probably for this reason that they are rare or absent on mountains and in moorland and marshland.

> ONE ESSENTIAL FOR HEDGEHOG WINTER SURVIVAL IS A GOOD SUPPLY OF LEAVES SUITABLE FOR MAKING A NEST

Hedgehogs are not strictly territorial. The free availability of their food means that they do not need to defend a supply area. However, they often fight if they do meet, one animal attempting to butt another and bowl it over—which suggests that they do have some sort of social hierarchy.

Many hedgehogs tend to forage for food in the same area night after night. In males, the home

FOCUS ON

ENGLISH SUBURBAN GARDEN

Hedgehogs are familiar nighttime visitors to gardens, attracted by a diverse habitat which often contains a greater concentration of insects than nearby fields and woods. Foraging in a smaller area saves the hedgehog precious energy.

For instance, an English suburban garden may have flower beds in one place, long grass in another, and a compost heap teeming with insects. The nooks and crannies often found beneath a garden shed provide warmth and shelter: the perfect site for a hedgehog's daytime nap.

However, gardens are not without their perils. Many hedgehogs die in burning piles of refuse, drown in garden ponds, or are killed when the long summer grass is mown.

A NIGHT'S WANDERINGS

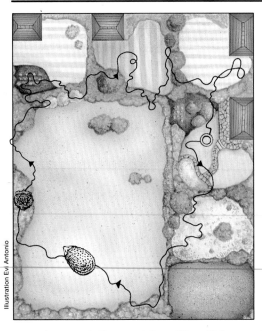

Illustration Evi Antonio

Hedgehogs are creatures of habit and return to the same foraging grounds night after night, covering a much broader territory than is usually imagined. On a typical night, a hedgehog will leave its nest at twilight and set out to visit as many different food sources as possible. These may include vegetable patches, orchards, woods, gardens, hedgerows, ponds, fields— and even houses in the hope of a saucer of food. The males range farther than the females—up to 2 miles (3 kilometers) from their starting point—and are less likely to return to their original starting point than to build another day nest elsewhere.

range is around 60 acres (about 20 to 30 hectares). This overlaps the ranges of several females, which are only around 25 acres (10 hectares).

With their larger home ranges, males are able to travel further and faster than females and, because of this extended traveling, male hedgehogs often do not return to the nest where they spent the previous day.

The size of the hedgehog's home range usually depends on the habitat: Hedgehogs in woodland areas move about less than those inhabiting more open places such as fields and parkland. ∎

NEIGHBORS

A surprising variety of wildlife shares the hedgehog's garden habitat. All of these creatures depend to some degree on the artificial environment created in towns and cities.

GRAY SQUIRREL

The town-dwelling squirrel eats nuts, bark, leaves, and roots but will also happily raid bird feeders and garbage cans.

EURASIAN ROBIN

In spite of its small size, the robin is fearless and will search for food in close proximity to people.

Illustrations Chris Christoforou

ENEMIES

RED FOX
Foxes hunt or scavenge at night, eating everything from hedge-hogs to discarded human food.

EUROPEAN BADGER
The powerful badger's sharp claws and pointed teeth can neatly peel a hedgehog.

TOAD

The toad is a nocturnal creature and has adapted to a garden environment, even breeding in garden ponds.

WOOD LOUSE

The wood louse lives in dark, damp places—under logs and stones—where it feeds on rotting wood and leaves.

TAWNY OWL

The tawny owl is a nocturnal hunter, with sharp eyes in the dark, good hearing, and soft wings for silent flight.

RABBIT

With its diet of grasses, herbs, shrubs, and roots, the rabbit crosses easily from meadowland to gardens.

PEACOCK BUTTERFLY

The peacock butterfly feeds on the nectar from buddleia flowers and hibernates in garden sheds.

FOOD AND FEEDING

Hedgehogs and tenrecs are insectivores—animals that eat mainly invertebrates (animals without bones such as insects, worms, and spiders)—but they take a wide variety of other prey. This includes small mammals such as mice, voles, shrews and moles, usually taken as babies, or carrion. Very occasionally hedgehogs eat snakes—their blood has a degree of immunity to adder venom and their spines stop snake fangs from puncturing the skin.

A MIXED BAG

Hedgehogs also eat other reptiles and amphibians, but these are more likely to be consumed as carrion than to be chased and killed. The chicks and eggs of ground-nesting birds may be a seasonal addition to the menu, as are, occasionally, berries and fallen fruit. In short, hedgehogs will eat almost anything edible that they can find, with a few notable exceptions: Their jaws are not strong enough to tackle snail shells, for instance. Hedgehogs also rarely eat centipedes—which can bite back—or grasshoppers—which probably move too fast for them to catch.

Although they have poor eyesight, hedgehogs have an excellent sense of smell, and can detect food with their flexible, moist nose under an inch or so (3 centimeters) of soil. Their hearing also plays an important role in detecting prey. Hedgehogs eat an average of 2.5 ounces (70 grams) of food a night and drink regularly, though a lot of moisture is obtained from their food.

The distributional ranges of different species of hedgehog tend not to overlap very much, and it is especially rare to find three species of hedgehog in the same geographical area. In contrast, all twenty

BATTLE OF WITS

This desert hedgehog (right) is bravely tackling a desert scorpion—its favorite food. Using stealth and speed, the hedgehog will bite off the stinger in the scorpion's tail before gobbling it up with great relish.

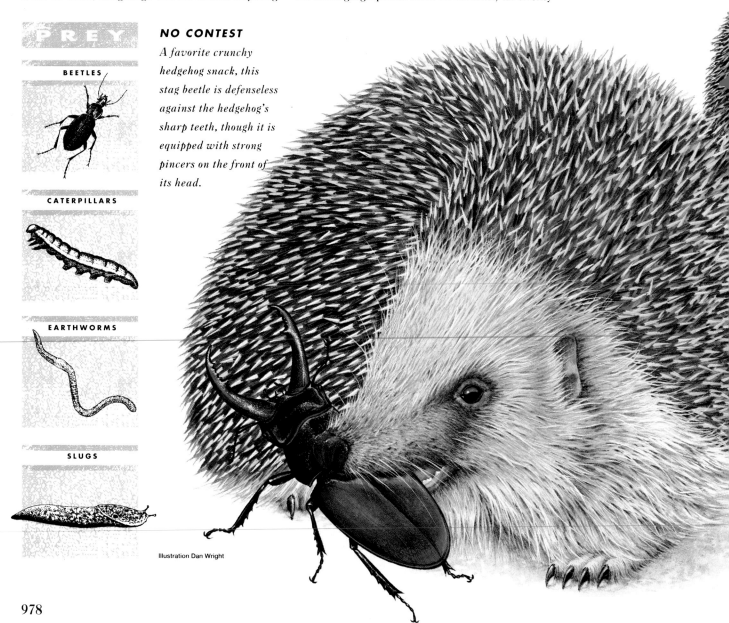

PREY

BEETLES

CATERPILLARS

EARTHWORMS

SLUGS

NO CONTEST

A favorite crunchy hedgehog snack, this stag beetle is defenseless against the hedgehog's sharp teeth, though it is equipped with strong pincers on the front of its head.

Illustration Dan Wright

species of tenrec share the one island of Madagascar. Yet they are able to live together because, although they are all basically insectivorous, many of them have come to specialize in certain kinds of invertebrates or to include other foods in their diet. This means that they compete less with one another. It is a rule of thumb that the two species cannot coexist on exactly the same resources.

In many cases food specializations among tenrecs have gone hand in hand with physical adaptations. The otterlike features of the aquatic tenrec help it to swim in the streams and rivers after

OUT OF ACTION

Various things can put hedgehogs out of action. They often fall into holes or pits and die. What they eat can be dangerous: The insects they favor may have been laced with pesticides by farmers or gardeners. They could fall prey to the hedgehog ringworm fungus, which causes bald patches, or to an attack of salmonella food poisoning.

Hedgehogs are also home to a variety of tiny insects, particularly fleas (see right)—one hedgehog may have over 1,000 fleas hidden among its spines! Usually the fleas do little harm, though their bites can attract blowflies whose larvae will attack their host.

HEDGEHOG FLEA

This flea lives mostly on hedgehogs, though it can occasionally be found on foxes or other animals.

TICK

The tick digs its mouth into the hedgehog's skin to suck its blood, then drops off after a while.

HEDGEHOG MITE

This microscopic insect burrows into skin and can cause anemia, weakness, and even death.

Illustrations Ruth Grewcock

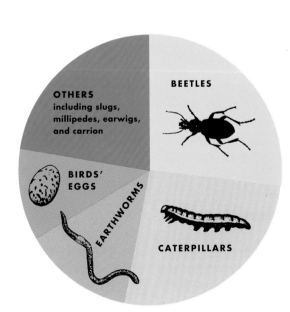

small frogs, fish, shrimp, crayfish, and insect larvae, and the stiff whiskers on its muzzle enable it to detect underwater vibrations made by its prey.

The land tenrecs have specialized in a number of ways. Because they can burrow like moles, rice tenrecs can exploit the invertebrates that live too deep in the soil for other tenrecs to reach. Streaked tenrecs have elongated snouts and a reduced number of delicate teeth, so they deal with their earthworm prey with ease.

A NICHE OF THEIR OWN

The omnivorous common tenrecs have the advantage of being bigger, so they can manage reptiles, frogs, and even small mammals. The lesser hedgehog tenrecs and long-tailed tenrecs spend much of their time in the trees, and this gives them access to lizards and nestling birds, which are not available to their ground-dwelling relatives. ■

OTHERS
including slugs, millipedes, earwigs, and carrion

BEETLES

BIRDS' EGGS

EARTHWORMS

CATERPILLARS

SPOILED FOR CHOICE

Of all the creatures that make up the hedgehog's diet, beetles and caterpillars seem to be eaten most often. Earthworms and birds' eggs are other popular options, followed by other invertebrate prey.

HIBERNATION

Hibernation is an effective way of conserving energy when food is scarce. As winter approaches and the weather gets colder, prey becomes more difficult to find and hedgehogs may use up more energy looking for food than they gain from eating it. When this happens, hedgehogs become inactive and use as little energy as possible until the weather and food supplies improve.

European hedgehogs may hibernate for up to five months, but during this time they wake, on average, once a week. They spend a day or two awake before returning to a state of hibernation.

UNDER COVER

One of the most important tasks for European hedgehogs is to build a nest, or "hibernaculum," which can withstand the winter weather. This is carefully constructed, usually under a pile of brushwood, a low bramble bush, or a garden shed. Hedgehogs may also occupy rabbit burrows, and in the colder parts of Europe they may even excavate their own burrows. Dry leaves are collected at night, pushed into a pile, and then the animal enters

 S I G H T

Jane Burton/Bruce Coleman Ltd.

SELF-ANOINTING

One unusual piece of hedgehog behavior that is difficult to explain involves the production of large quantities of frothy saliva which the hedgehog smears all over its back and spines until its body appears to be covered with soapsuds.

This practice is called self-anointing and is often triggered by smelling or chewing astringent substances, such as leather, varnish, cigar butts, or toad skin. Its function is a mystery: It is not part of the normal grooming behavior, nor is there any evident effect on the resident flea population. One theory is that the spines become coated with a mild poison that enhances their protective function, or it may be that the saliva contains a sexually attractive odor.

the heap and shuffles around inside. The leafy walls of the nest provide effective insulation, protecting against extreme cold as well as brief warm spells, which might wake the animal up unnecessarily.

Keeping the body warm is one of the most energy-consuming of activities so, to counteract this, hedgehogs allow their body temperature to fall to that of their surroundings. At low body temperatures all the normal bodily functions slow right down: The heart rate slows from around 190 to less than 20 beats per minute and several minutes may elapse between breaths. These changes save on

Illustration Toni Hargreaves

CURLING UP

When in danger, hedgehogs may contract their muscles and roll up into a defensive ball; they have specially modified vertebrae that enable them to do this.

First, a pair of muscles pulls the loose skin forward over the head, and another pair pulls it backward over the animal's bottom. Then a big circular muscle that runs all the way around the animal's body operates like the drawstring of a duffel bag. As it contracts, it draws the spiny skin downward and closes it tight, forcing the legs, head, and tail inside. The result is a tightly contracted ball, completely enveloped in the spiny skin.

energy expenditure so effectively that it is reduced to one-fiftieth of the normal requirement, but at the price of complete immobility and major changes in body chemistry that cannot be swiftly reversed.

TAKING IT EASY

Many tenrecs, such as the large-eared and common tenrecs, adopt a similar strategy. They conserve energy when foraging is difficult by becoming torpid. Their temperature drops and their metabolism is reduced. They spend anything from a few days to six months in this state, depending on the food supply. Four-toed and desert hedgehogs save energy by estivating—remaining dormant during the hot, dry season—deep in cool burrows. Tropical hedgehogs do not need to hibernate or estivate at all, because food is available all year round.

During hibernation the hedgehog's fuel supply comes from the mass of "white fat" stored below the skin, which may comprise a third of the total body weight at the beginning of hibernation. This precious store is used up over the course of winter.

> IF PLENTY OF FOOD IS AVAILABLE, THERE IS NO NEED FOR HIBERNATION—EVEN DURING THE WINTER

In addition, large orange-colored lobes of "brown fat" below the skin around the shoulder generate heat when the animal wants to warm up and resume normal activity. Before it hibernates, the hedgehog must have accumulated enough white fat to last for many weeks and enough brown fat to enable it to wake up several times, otherwise hibernation will simply be a prelude to death—as it proves to be for many young or underfed animals. ∎

K E Y F A C T S

● Generally hedgehogs need to weigh about 1 lb (454 g) before hibernation to be fat enough to survive a normal winter.

● When hibernating, hedgehogs allow their body temperature to fall from 95°F (35°C) to 50°F (10°C) or less.

● The heart rate of a hibernating hedgehog drops way down, from 190 to 20 beats a minute.

LIFE CYCLE

In Europe hedgehogs breed from about April to September, with the main period of activity in May and June when the nights are warm. Second litters may be born, but most arrive too late to survive the oncoming winter. Tenrecs usually wait for the wet season, when invertebrate numbers are greatest, but most tropical hedgehogs can breed for much of the year, because there is always food

RAISING A FAMILY PUTS A GREAT STRAIN ON A FEMALE HEDGEHOG'S RESOURCES, SO THE BREEDING SEASON MUST COINCIDE WITH A TIME WHEN FOOD IS PLENTIFUL

available. For the desert-dwelling long-eared and desert hedgehogs, there is only enough food to raise a single family between July and September.

During the breeding season, a male European hedgehog will court any female he meets by circling around her. She will usually rebuff him by turning

NEWBORN
young are tiny, blind, and helpless. Their pink skin soon begins to shrink and their soft, white spines eventually start to poke through.

BY FLATTENING HER SPINES
and stretching her body out flat, the female makes mating easier for the male who mounts her from behind.

AMAZING FACTS

Mark Pidgeon/Oxford Scientific Films

BABY BOOM

The common tenrec can have up to 32 young at a time, which is the largest family produced by any mammal. Females have up to 29 teats with which to suckle a litter.

With so many young to support, the mother and her offspring often need to carry on foraging for food through the night and well into the daytime.

Because it is so dangerous for young tenrecs to be moving about in daylight, they are camouflaged with a striped coat of spines that they lose with later molts.

GROWING UP
The life of a young European hedgehog

TWO DAYS OLD

After a couple of days, the typical brown spines of the adults begin to appear here and there among the white spines.

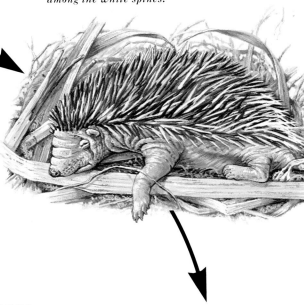

BABY HEDGEHOGS

When they are about eleven days old, the babies start to experiment with rolling up into a ball. Their eyes open after fourteen days.

IN SINGLE FILE,

youngsters follow their mother on a nighttime foraging expedition, keeping close together.

FROM BIRTH TO DEATH

EUROPEAN HEDGEHOG

GESTATION: ABOUT 34 DAYS	**MOBILITY:** 3 WEEKS
LITTER SIZE: 2–7; USUALLY 4 OR 5	**WEANING:** 4–6 WEEKS
BREEDING: SEASONAL; BETWEEN APRIL AND SEPTEMBER	**SEXUAL MATURITY:** 1 YEAR
WEIGHT AT BIRTH: 1 OZ (28 G)	**INDEPENDENCE:** 4–6 WEEKS
EYES OPEN: 14 DAYS	**LONGEVITY:** 3–5 YEARS; MAXIMUM ABOUT 10 YEARS

to keep her flank toward him, all the while puffing and snorting, so that the couple repeatedly shuffle around and around in circles.

If the female allows the male to mate her, he will do so from behind. The female's spines are very slippery, so the male holds on to the spines on her shoulder with his teeth. There is no pair bond between the male and female, and the male takes no part in rearing the young.

> ONE-FIFTH OF ALL HEDGEHOGS DIE IN THEIR FIRST MONTH BECAUSE THE MOTHER CANNOT PRODUCE ENOUGH MILK

The female builds a nest using dry leaves or grasses in a sheltered spot and, after about thirty-four days, four or five blind, pink, and helpless babies arrive. They are fed on milk from the mother's five pairs of nipples. When they are about three weeks old, the mother leads her family out of the nest each night to look for food. The young become independent of their mother at about four to six weeks of age. The family then disperses to lead solitary lives.

DIFFICULT TIMES

Over half the hedgehogs born never see their first birthday. During the autumn, they must increase their weight eighteen times from birth to survive hibernation. Animals smaller than this do not have enough fat to get through to the following season.

Hedgehogs that do survive their first hibernation stand a fair chance of living another two or three years. However, every winter is a fresh hazard and only about 30 percent of adult hedgehogs survive from one year to the next. For the hedgehog "old age" is about five years and the maximum age is likely to be about ten years. ∎

Illustrations Toni Hargreaves

NOWHERE TO HIDE

THE MODERN WORLD CAN BE A DANGEROUS PLACE FOR HEDGEHOGS— INTENSIVE FARMING TECHNIQUES, URBAN EXPANSION, AND THE AUTOMOBILE ALL PRESENT PROBLEMS FOR THIS POPULAR CREATURE

Food shortages and the vulnerability presented by the need to hibernate are probably the most common natural threats to the survival of individual hedgehogs and tenrecs.

As a species, however, the greatest danger to their continued healthy existence comes almost exclusively from the activities of humans. Unfortunately, it is difficult to assess how great such threats are as so little is known about the current status of hedgehog and tenrec populations.

NEW METHODS

Changes in farming methods come at the forefront of these threats. Much of the world's pastureland, so rich in the worms and insects on which the hedgehog thrives, has been turned into fields for grain and other crops. This arable farmland is often treated with chemicals designed specifically to kill the very creatures hedgehogs need for food.

Some pesticides are very persistent and are accumulated by predators from tiny quantities in

> THE FACT THAT SOME PESTICIDES ACCUMULATE IN FAT MEANS THEY ARE PARTICULARLY DANGEROUS TO HIBERNATING HEDGEHOGS

their prey. Hedgehogs eating contaminated beetles, for example, could build up significant levels of harmful organochlorine residues in their body, sometimes leading to sterility or even death. Such chemicals accumulate in fat and, because fat is so important to hibernating hedgehogs, they may be especially vulnerable.

Even when harmful chemicals are not in use, hedgehogs still face a major problem on modern farms. Whereas old pasture offered food and shelter (in clumps of weed or odd corners), arable land is plowed up every year, harvested, and then left to lie bare and open until the new crop grows. Though the removal of hedgerows, copses, and odd patches of waste ground increases the ease and efficiency of arable farming by creating bigger fields, it deprives hedgehogs of vital winter nest sites. Such changes have occurred over large areas of countryside in the past twenty or thirty years.

POTENTIAL DANGERS

Farmers are not the only users of dangerous chemicals. Gardeners, though on a smaller scale, also use quantities of pesticides—with similar potential dangers. Slug pellets, for example, are dangerous to children and pets as well as hedgehogs and should never be left in heaps where many could be eaten at once. To lessen this risk, the pellets are

Hedgehogs can benefit from the waste produced by human society and are a common sight in many towns and cities.

John Daniels/Ardea

Hans Reinhard/Bruce Coleman Ltd.

*The graph below details the number of hedgehogs
deliberately killed in Britain since 1960.*

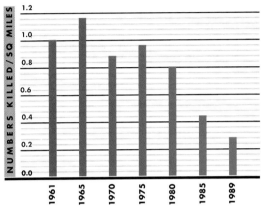

**The number of British hedgehogs killed
deliberately has fallen steadily since World
War II. Gamekeepers, once the hedgehog's
most fearsome enemy, are now a rarer
breed, and the public image of the
hedgehog is generally much more positive.
On the other hand, the real reason for the
decline in kills may be due to an overall
decline in the native hedgehog population.**

generally hard, distasteful, and colored blue—all
factors intended to reduce their attractiveness to
mammals and garden birds. However, there is also
the chance that hedgehogs and other animals might
eat slugs that have already been poisoned and
consequently, in doing so, poison themselves.

Long grass sprayed with weed killer is a
dangerous place for hedgehogs to forage at night.
Although sprays are not often used on the ground

THOUGH HEDGEHOGS ARE PROTECTED
BY LAW IN MANY EUROPEAN COUNTRIES,
SUCH LEGISLATION OFFERS ONLY
LIMITED PROTECTION

where hedgehogs will come into contact with them,
they may still spread into the soil from plants and
shrubs. Here they contaminate the hedgehog's food
supplies together with those of garden birds,
amphibians, and other wildlife.

While hedgehogs do have limited legal protection
in many parts of Europe, the law is incapable of
protecting them from threats such as habitat loss,
changes in farming methods, and the effects of
agricultural and garden chemicals. Once, however,

the hedgehog had no protection at all and was regarded as nothing more than vermin. In the year 1566, for instance, Queen Elizabeth I of England passed a law for the "Preservation of Grayne," which condemned hedgehogs as well as "noxious birds and vermin."

STATUTORY PESTS

Their destruction was to be encouraged by churchwardens paying a bounty for each one killed in their parish. The Act was repealed only in 1863, meaning that, in England at least, hedgehogs were a statutory pest for almost three hundred years.

For a long time, gamekeepers held hedgehogs responsible for losses of pheasant and partridge eggs. In the 1930s, such country "wisdom" was turned on its head when studies showed that hedgehogs were rarely responsible for such activities, which were far more likely to be carried out by foxes, dogs, and cats.

THE RISE IN ROAD TRAFFIC PRESENTS A HIGHLY VISIBLE THREAT—TWO TO THREE MILLION HEDGEHOGS DIE EVERY YEAR UNDER THE WHEELS OF A CAR

Nowadays, hedgehogs are rarely killed deliberately, though humans can still make life very difficult for them. In Denmark, for example—which is one of Europe's more ecologically committed countries—surveys suggest that between 70,000 and 100,000 hedgehogs are run over by automobiles every year.

In fact, it has been estimated that two to three million hedgehogs are killed every year on the world's roads. In some parts of Germany it is claimed that whole local populations have been wiped out—innocent victims of the postwar world's love affair with the automobile.

MOWED DOWN

Judging by the numbers of badly injured hedgehogs found in summer, lawn mowers are another modern hazard. Local authorities mow roadsides to keep weeds under control and reduce fire risks but, in doing so, destroy hedgehogs and the sorts of places where they spend their summer days.

Some modern lawn mowers are particularly dangerous as they are designed to give access to odd corners and crannies, ideal locations for nesting hedgehog mothers. As a result, hedgehogs sustain serious wounds and may even be killed outright.

At the moment, the European hedgehog is still a fairly common animal, and in the 20th century it even expanded its range northward to Finland.

Edwin Mickleburgh/Survival Anglia

ENDANGERED ENVIRONMENT

THE DECLINE OF THE BRITISH HEDGEROW

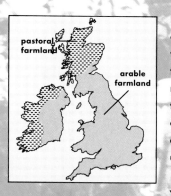

pastoral farmland

arable farmland

Rural areas are often thought to be free from the interfering hands of modern humans. In truth, however, the countryside is often as artificial as any urban environment.

Britain was the world's first industrial nation, and it developed its early industries by moving thousands of people from the countryside into the booming manufacturing towns. In order to feed these new urban populations, agriculture became more intensive, a process that has continued to the present day.

COMMON LEGACY

One of the legacies of the early agricultural revolution was the hedgerow, once a common sight in rural and semi-rural Britain. Hedgerows, as their name suggests, were rows of hedges and bushes that divided fields and pastures set aside for different purposes. Hedgerows were to prove a boon for certain small mammals and birds, the hedgehog included, which nested and foraged there in relative security.

New farming methods, developed in the 1960s, placed the hedgerow under threat. Huge amalgamated fields became the order of the day, where single arable

CONSERVATION MEASURES

Europe leads the world in hedgehog conservation, though, all too often, legislation fails to address the crucial issue of loss of habitat.

● In Britain, the Wildlife and Countryside Act of 1981 granted a degree of legal protection to the hedgehog, bringing British law into line with most other European Community members.

crops could be cultivated, reaping large profits. Hedgerows, traditionally used to separate fields, became superfluous.

A further problem was caused by the growth in intensive animal rearing that did away with great tracts of pastoral land, the stronghold of the hedgerow.

In recent years, however, the decline in hedgerows has been checked to a certain extent, as farmers have been encouraged to replant them on their land.

A more pressing problem now, though, is urban development. The expansion of towns, highways, and reservoirs into land once used for agriculture results in loss of habitat for wildlife.

INTENSIVE FARMING USING MODERN TECHNOLOGY HAS LITTLE NEED FOR THE HUMBLE HEDGEROW.

● Hedgehog Rescue Stations have recently been established in several European countries to care for sick and injured animals. The British Hedgehog Preservation Society was established in 1982 to promote the conservation of hedgehogs and to encourage education in wildlife matters. A similar organization, known as Pro-Igel, has also been established in Switzerland.

HEDGEHOGS IN DANGER

THE CHART BELOW SHOWS HOW THE INTERNATIONAL UNION FOR THE CONSERVATION OF NATURE (IUCN), OR THE WORLD CONSERVATION UNION, CLASSIFIES THE STATUS OF SOME SPECIES OF HEDGEHOG:

SOUTH AFRICAN HEDGEHOG	RARE
MINDANAO MOONRAT	VULNERABLE

VULNERABLE MEANS THE SPECIES IS LIKELY TO BECOME ENDANGERED IF THINGS CONTINUE AS THEY ARE. ENDANGERED MEANS THE ANIMAL'S SURVIVAL IS UNLIKELY UNLESS STEPS ARE TAKEN TO SAVE IT. RARE MEANS A SPECIES IS AT RISK BUT NOT YET ENDANGERED OR VULNERABLE.

Despite this, its populations have probably dropped considerably over the last century or so, as pasture-land and other suitable hedgehog habitats have been lost to other uses.

Cases such as that of the African hedgehog, *Atelerix frontalis*, are causing concern. Popular as a pet and as a food source, the African hedgehog has

THE SPREAD OF THE SAHARA DESERT IS ISOLATING POPULATIONS OF THE DESERT HEDGEHOG, LEAVING THEM VULNERABLE TO NATURAL DISASTERS

lost much of its habitat of open grassland and scrub to agriculture. The situation is so bad that the creature is now listed as "rare" and appears on Appendix II of CITES.

Increased desertification in the Sahara and Arabian Deserts is fragmenting populations of the desert hedgehog. Habitat loss breaks up the range of a species, leaving populations isolated from one another. As a result, individual populations become too small to survive. At the very least, they are more vulnerable to natural disasters or further habitat encroachment. The Egyptian subspecies is already extremely scarce, if not extinct.

THE ELUSIVE TENREC

Assessing tenrec populations is even more difficult than counting hedgehogs, as they are generally rather small and elusive, and little is known of their nocturnal habits. Some species don't seem to have been affected too badly by the expansion of the human population. For example, the greater

ALONGSIDE MAN

A HELPING HAND

Urban hedgehogs owe much of their success to food put out for them by European householders. Extra food is vital in the autumn to help underweight animals build up sufficient fat reserves to last the winter.

However, the most common offerings, bread and milk, are the worst possible foods for hedgehogs—cow's milk gives them diarrhea, and bread also disagrees with them. They should be given canned cat or dog food—they are particularly fond of the liver-flavored ones—or sardines.

Owen Newman/Oxford Scientific Films

hedgehog tenrec is commonly found feeding from town garbage cans, while the lesser hedgehog tenrec prefers to forage around the huts of small villages. The streaked tenrec also seems to benefit from man-made habitats. It nests and sleeps in planted

Many gardeners adopt hedgehogs as free-ranging pets as they rid gardens of slugs and other pests.

FOREST CLEARANCE IN MADAGASCAR, CAUSED BY THE EVER-GROWING HUMAN POPULATION, THREATENS TO DESTROY THE TENREC'S HABITAT

---

eucalyptus groves, and feeds by night on the worms that abound in nearby rice paddies. Most tenrecs are, however, sensitive to the changes brought about by mankind, particularly loss of habitat. As the banks of streams and the shores of marshes are colonized or cleared for agriculture, the aquatic

Thousands of hedgehogs are killed every year in bonfires. Nesting mothers, unaware of the dangers, use brush piles as shelters for their young.

tenrec loses feeding areas and safe nest sites.

Forest clearance threatens the homes of species such as the long-tailed tenrec and also increases the loss of topsoil into streams and rivers. Consequently, rivers silt up and soon become uninhabitable for aquatic tenrecs. In addition, the loss of topsoil deprives other creatures of the worms and insects it formerly supported.

NEW ARRIVALS

Many of the long-tailed tenrecs are being squeezed out by newer, more aggressive arrivals to Madagascar, such as the oriental house shrew and the black rat. These animals arrived with the early colonists, stowed away on boats and in cargo. They are adaptable creatures, breeding quickly and prolifically, and compete with the slower breeding, more specialized tenrecs for food and nest sites.

THOUGH THE TENREC LACKS EFFECTIVE LEGAL PROTECTION IN ITS NATURAL ENVIRONMENT, ITS PLIGHT HAS COME TO THE ATTENTION OF ECOLOGISTS

Unfortunately, tenrecs are not effectively protected in Madagascar, although the IUCN does list the aquatic tenrec as "vulnerable." However, like the laws created to protect the European hedgehog, this does not address the problem of loss of habitat faced by the animal in its natural environment.

Ironically, the common tenrec is considered a pest in Mauritius, where it has been introduced. There it attacks chickens and has probably contributed to the rarity—and even extinction—of native species unique to that island, such as the dodo. ∎

Robert Harvey/Survival Anglia

INTO THE FUTURE

For most species of tenrec, the main threat to the future lies in habitat destruction. This is a major problem throughout Madagascar, where much of the vast ancient rain forest has been cleared. Unfortunately, habitat destruction seems unlikely to be controlled except in a few areas set aside as national parks or nature reserves. Since tenrecs are poorly studied, elusive, and often scarce, it may be hard to discover what is happening to them until long after they have disappeared.

CONCLUSIVE EVIDENCE

In thick forest habitat, the fact that an animal hasn't been seen for ten years or more is not necessarily evidence that it is extinct. Yet if it isn't seen for a long time, by the time people become aware of its existence and take action, it may be too late.

Most hedgehogs seem to have a reasonably secure future, as enough areas of their habitat seem

PREDICTION

The greatest threat to the long-term future of the hedgehog, along with many other small mammals and birds, lies with the spread of large-scale chemical farming. Huge expanses of arable land, devoted to the cultivation of just one particular grain, provide few niches for wild animals and flowers. Road building, the spread of industry, and continuing urban expansion are also formidable threats.

likely to remain largely unspoiled for some years to come. The loss of pasture to create arable farmland, so destructive to wildlife, may be past its peak. New rules within the European Community encourage agricultural land to be set aside to reduce overproduction in grain. This may result in the creation of more land suitable for hedgehogs.

THE BIG SQUEEZE

It is unlikely, however, that hedgehog numbers in most of Europe will increase, due to intensive house- and road-building programs. Along with a lot of other wild animals, the hedgehog is likely to be squeezed hard in years to come as a result of the expansion of our own all-too-numerous species. ■

A GROWING PROBLEM

Hedgehogs do not make happy pets. Taking in an underweight juvenile before winter may well save its life, but it should always be released the following spring. Most of our traditional pets come from generations of captive animals and are accustomed to the confinement we impose on them. This is not the case for hedgehogs. While it is beneficial for free-ranging hedgehogs to receive extra food from humans, many remain restless and distressed when forced into captivity.

Hedgehogs are also very messy, rather smelly, and are not particularly entertaining pets, as their nocturnal nature ensures that their best moments are often missed by human observers. Despite these drawbacks, in recent years a hedgehog pet trade has burgeoned in the United States, where some of the rarer species are believed to fetch as much as $250.

A NEW ALLIANCE

The hedgehog has, rather unwittingly, discovered a new ally—the golfer. Golf is a booming business throughout the world, and there are now almost 3,000 golf courses in Britain alone. These are essentially re-creations of the grassland and heathland of Scotland in which the game originated. Such environments provide an ideal home for creatures like the hedgehog. Barriers to the golfer's performance, such as the rough or the bunkers, are particularly attractive. However, a growing number of environmentalists, particularly in Southeast Asia, have raised questions about the overall ecological impact of the golf craze.

Graham Allen/Linden Artists

HIPPOPOTAMUSES

RELATIONS

The hippopotamus and pygmy hippopotamus belong to the suborder Suiformes. Other members of this suborder include:

PIGS

PECCARIES

WHITE-LIPPED PECCARY

DOMESTIC PIG

AFRICAN BUSHPIG

BABIRUSA

WARTHOG

Aiken/ZEFA

The hippos are classed with the pigs and peccaries in the suborder Suiformes, within the Artiodactyla order of even-toed ungulates. The two hippo genera each contain only one species. The pygmy hippo is listed in the genus Choeropsis, but some taxonomists suggest reclassification to Hexaprotodon, to reflect a link with a number of primitive, now-extinct hippos.

ORDER

Artiodactyla

SUBORDER

Suina

HIPPO GENUS

Hippopotamus

SPECIES

amphibius

PYGMY HIPPO GENUS

Choeropsis

SPECIES

liberiensis

LITTLE AND LARGE

THE HIPPO IS A LOT LARGER THAN ITS RELATIVE, THE PYGMY HIPPO—BUT THIS IS ONLY ONE OF SEVERAL DIFFERENCES BETWEEN THE TWO SPECIES. IN TRUTH, THEY ARE AS ALIKE AS APPLES AND ORANGES

A bloodred sun sinks on the horizon, spreading a tinge of crimson-gold over the rippling grasses beyond the lakeshore. Flies dance among the swaying reeds. Silently, a pair of fleshy nostrils break the lake's surface—then the peace is shattered by an explosion of hot breath and glittering spray as an immense pink mound erupts from the depths. Roused from tranquil submersion, a common hippo is emerging for a twilight bout of grazing.

The common hippopotamus, or just plain "hippo," is the only species of its genus. It spends its days wallowing in the waterways of sub-Saharan Africa and its nights cropping the lush grasses nearby. And it is huge. An adult bull can weigh more than three tons and equal a station wagon in length; its head alone can weigh nearly half a ton. The barrel-like body sits on stumpy legs with dainty, four-toed feet, but the hippo is no slouch: It can power up steep banks and, on the flat, can outrun a man.

The pygmy hippo resembles a scaled-down hippo, though with a more rounded muzzle and less prominent eyes. It lives a secret life in West Africa's moist forests and is rarely seen. There were fleeting glimpses of it from the first recorded sighting in 1844 to 1980, when most of our knowledge on the species was gathered.

OBSCURE BEGINNINGS

The earliest fossil records for the common hippo date from the later years of the Miocene epoch (25–5 million years ago). However, unraveling the hippo's ancestry prior to this time involves a lot of educated guesswork. Hippos probably evolved either from pigs and peccaries, or from a now-extinct group known as anthracotheres (ANN-thrack-o-theers)—piglike animals with long, low skull, and four-toed feet.

The anthracotheres lived by streams and rivers, as the hippo does today. But the evidence for their ancestry is based mainly upon *Merycopotamus* (Meh-ree-ko-POT-ah-muss), an anthracothere of a couple of million years ago, whose skull bears hippolike features. And since *Merycopotamus* appeared later than the hippos, it may not be an ancestor, but simply a parallel species with a similar lifestyle. More fossils may yet be found that support the anthracothere ancestry—but without such evidence, the Miocene pigs and peccaries deserve equal credit as the hippo's forebears.

Over the last five or six million years, several hippo species lived and died out in Africa, with relatives also in Asia until just a few thousand years ago. Fossils suggest that some of these extinct hippos

M. B. England/Ardea

Anthony Bannister/Oxford Scientific Films

The pygmy hippo (above) *is shy and reclusive, preferring its own company to that of other hippos.*

 **SIGHT**

SPECIES PAIRS

Despite their superficial similarity, the hippo and pygmy hippo share few other features. Apart from the obvious difference in size, they also have different jaws. Up to 20 in (50 cm) wide, the hippo's jaws are ideal for cropping grasses, as well as providing anchorage for its impressive dental weaponry. The pygmy hippo's neater muzzle is better equipped to browse from trees and shrubs in the forest.

The hippo frequents the waterways among savanna and grassland; the pygmy hippo skulks in the rain forest. This unusual phenomenon—of two physically similar species with very different lifestyles—is known as a species pair.

A similar example might be the red fox and the arctic fox. Physically, these animals are much alike, but both have adapted to exploit very different habitats.

were more advanced even than today's pygmy hippo, so the pygmy hippo—for which there exists no fossil record—may represent a living relict of the modern hippo's ancestors.

Early hippos, like the pygmy hippo, probably had sun-sensitive skin and also used shaded forest streams as a refuge. Over the last 15 million years or more, however, the climate and vegetation of Africa have been shifting repeatedly from one extreme to another; as the forests shrank, hippos would have eventually been forced into more open habitats. They gained new food sources when great stretches of grassland opened up, but they could not cope with living exclusively on land. So instead of making a major physical adjustment, hippos changed their behavior—grazing by night and retreating, by day, to the cool comfort of water.

IT'S ALL IN THE HEAD

The hippo's amphibious equipment includes a specialized skull. The massive cranium tapers sharply along the muzzle, then widens again at the snout to accommodate the tusklike canines and peglike incisors. The hippo uses these canines for attack and defense, thrusting, ramming, and slashing them into an adversary, since in the water any more agile

In contrast to its smaller relative, the hippo lives in large, noisy groups.

method of fighting would be impossible. To exploit its weaponry to the fullest, the hippo uses thick muscles in the jowl to open the jaws to 150 degrees. And to keep its heavy lower jaw out of the water, its neck jackknifes steeply upward. With just such a "yawn" on his face, a bull hippo can go confidently into battle, for a special neck joint ensures that the heavy shocks sustained head-on by the jaws are cushioned by the full length of the backbone.

The facial features themselves can be compared with those of crocodiles or frogs. The ears, eyes, and nostrils sit high on the head, enabling a submerged hippo to stay fully in touch with the outside world. When diving, the hippo uses muscles to seal off the nostrils and tuck down the ears. Significantly, the eyes of the pygmy hippo are set lower on the skull sides. This supports the idea that the pygmy hippo is fairly primitive in evolutionary terms, pointing back in history to a time when hippos generally spent more time in the forests than in the water.

SUNTAN LOTION

In both hippo species, special skin glands ooze a sticky fluid all over the body. In certain lights the fluid appears red, which led to an earlier belief that hippos could literally sweat blood. Far from being blood, the alkaline goo contains a pigment that filters out the sun's harmful rays. When a hippo leaves the water during the day, the fluid dries off to a hard lacquer, which protects the sensitive skin from burning. The fluid also seems to disinfect flesh wounds, even in the filthiest wallows. However, the hippo lacks sweat glands—or, for that matter, any physical means for body cooling. As a result, it keeps to water temperatures in the region of 65–95°F (18–35°C). ∎

ⒶNCESTORS
GIANT OF THE PAST

Stratified fossil deposits in a Tanzanian gorge, spanning a period of 1.8–0.3 million years ago, can be pieced together to reveal a "byline" of now-extinct hippo forms. As they evolved, these hippos became larger, with increasingly higher eye sockets and longer skulls. They culminated in *Hippopotamus gorgops*, whose eyes protruded on stalks and enabled the animal to submerge almost fully and still view its surroundings. While *H. gorgops* is not a true ancestor of today's hippo, it gives us a rare insight into how land mammals evolved to cope with an aquatic life.

Color illustrations Richard Tibbs

THE HIPPOS' FAMILY TREE

The hippos are even-toed ungulates (hoofed, grazing mammals). Ungulates first appeared 65 million years ago and have diversified widely. Both hippos are associated with the pigs and peccaries of the suborder Suiformes, owing to certain physiological affinities and a likely common ancestry. Of the several hippo species that have become extinct, some enjoyed a wide distribution over Eurasia, even living in England between the most recent ice ages.

PYGMY HIPPO

Hexaprotodon liberiensis
(Heck-sa-PRO-to-don lib-eh-REE-en-sis)

Hidden away for thousands of years in the rain forests of Liberia, Sierra Leone, and other West African countries, the pygmy hippo was not known to zoologists in any great detail until the mid-1980s. Dramatically smaller than its relative, the pygmy hippo is also much rarer. It lives at low densities and exhibits few social bonds, reacting to intrusion by rushing off into thickets.

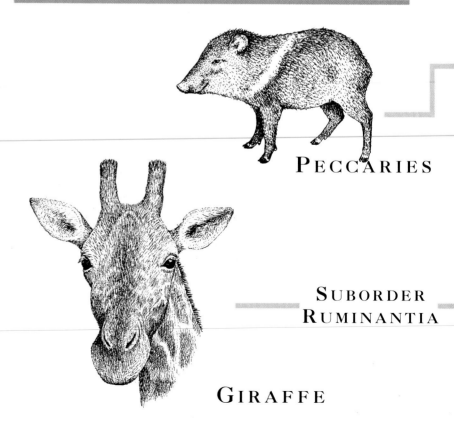

PECCARIES

SUBORDER
RUMINANTIA

GIRAFFE

HIPPO

Hippopotamus amphibius
(hip-o-POT-a-mus
am-FIB-ee-us)

The truly amphibious hippo has been known to humanity since the earliest times. Linked by the ancient Egyptians with a fertility goddess, it fared less favorably with the Romans, who exploited it cruelly in their circuses. Today, it continues to harass African farmers with its capacity for ruining crops, but to many people it represents one of the most enduring sights of the savanna.

PIGS

CAMELS

SUBORDER
SUIFORMES

SUBORDER
TYLOPODA

PRIMITIVE
UNGULATES

ODD-TOED
UNGULATES

ALL UNGULATES

ANATOMY: THE HIPPOPOTAMUS

The pygmy hippo is roughly the size and shape of a prize pig; it may reach a length of 5.7 ft (1.75 m), stand up to 3.3 ft (1 m) at the shoulder, and weigh up to 600 lb (275 kg). The hippo is closer in length and weight to a small truck (see Fact File): An adult bull may weigh over three tons. Female hippos are smaller than the males.

FEET

On both species, each foot has four spreading, conical toes connected by small webs. A pad of tissue on the heel helps to brace the structure. The pygmy hippo's toes are smaller and more slender than those of its relative. The feet suit soft soil or mud and are not very useful for walking great distances on firm ground.

PYGMY HIPPO

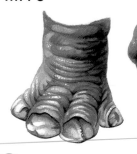

HIPPO

THE SKIN

in both species is protected from infection and sunburn by the secretion of a pink, viscous fluid that hardens to a lacquer when exposed to the air. The outer skin is thin and loses moisture rapidly when not immersed in water.

THE EYES

give good vision both in and out of the water. Night vision is adequate. Placed high on the skull, the eyes act as "periscopes" when the hippo's torso is immersed.

THE EARS

constantly waggle to flick away flies. The hippo can tuck them down to keep water out when submerged.

X RAY

The sturdy spine and stout legs form a crude arch, which supports the immense weight of the body. The neck vertebrae take the tension produced by the weight of the head; the spinal/cranial link in particular is heavily reinforced. The hippo's bulk obliges it to take the weight off its feet regularly—either by immersion or by lying prone.

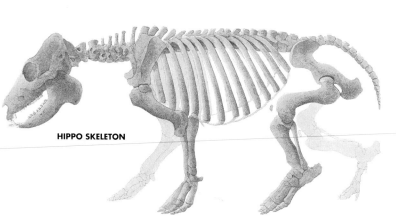

HIPPO SKELETON

The hippo's dentition is dominated by the curving, tusklike lower canines, which can grow up to 20 in (50 cm) in length. They grow constantly, but their tips are honed by constant jawing. Of the four incisors in the lower jaw, the inner pair are particularly long and peglike. The canines and incisors are smaller in the upper jaw. The molars are simple and low-crowned, for grinding food.

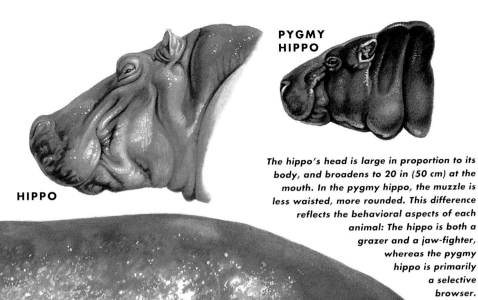

PYGMY HIPPO

HIPPO

The hippo's head is large in proportion to its body, and broadens to 20 in (50 cm) at the mouth. In the pygmy hippo, the muzzle is less waisted, more rounded. This difference reflects the behavioral aspects of each animal: The hippo is both a grazer and a jaw-fighter, whereas the pygmy hippo is primarily a selective browser.

FACT FILE

THE HIPPOPOTAMUS

CLASSIFICATION

GENUS: *HIPPOPOTAMUS*

SPECIES: *AMPHIBIUS*

SIZE

HEAD–BODY LENGTH/MALE: 10–16.4 FT (3–5 M)

HEAD–BODY LENGTH/FEMALE: 9.5–14 FT (2.9–4.3 M)

TAIL LENGTH: 15 IN (40 CM)

SHOULDER HEIGHT: 4.9–5.4 FT (150–165 CM)

WEIGHT/MALE: 1,100–7,000 LB (500–3,200 KG)

AVERAGE: 3,250 LB (1,475 KG)

WEIGHT/FEMALE: 1,450–5,170 LB (650–2,350 KG)

AVERAGE: 3,000 LB (1,360 KG)

COLORATION

PURPLE-GRAY TO BLUE-BLACK ABOVE, BROWNISH PINK BELOW AND AROUND EYES AND EARS. OCCASIONALLY PARTIAL ALBINO (BRIGHT PINK WITH LIVER BLOTCHES). FACIAL PIGMENTATION MAY VARY AMONG INDIVIDUALS

FEATURES

MASSIVE, BARREL-LIKE TRUNK, HAIRLESS AND OFTEN HEAVILY SCARRED FROM FIGHTS

SHORT LEGS WITH SPREADING, FOUR-TOED FEET

STUMPY, ALMOST HAIRLESS TAIL

LARGE, HOURGLASS HEAD WITH WIDE, FLESHY SNOUT

EYES, EARS, AND NOSTRILS POSITIONED HIGH ON HEAD

DISTINCTIVE PINK SECRETION OVER HIDE, PARTICULARLY DURING TIMES OF HIGH EXCITEMENT

THE LEGS

are short and columnlike. They are surprisingly sturdy, enabling the hippo to walk along the riverbed or to gallop on land at up to 30 mph (48 km/h).

BODY AND HIDE

Characteristically barrel-shaped body. The hide is up to 2.5 in (6 cm) thick around the hindquarters but is much thinner around the forequarters.

THE TAIL

is short, stumpy, and almost hairless. The hippo wags it rapidly when defecating to scatter dung over a 6.5 ft (2 m) area.

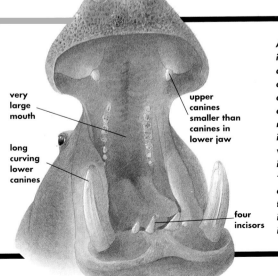

very large mouth

upper canines smaller than canines in lower jaw

long curving lower canines

four incisors

Although the braincase itself is small, the bony masses around the base of the skull are heavily reinforced. They are uniquely formed to make a sturdy lock with the first neck vertebra when the skull is fully raised, for example when the teeth are exposed in combat. The narrow "waist" of the skull accommodates the cheek teeth, while the front section is widened to hold the incisors and canines.

HIPPO SKULL

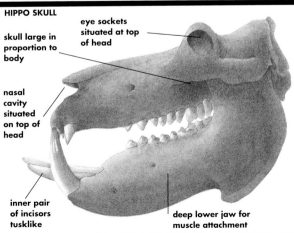

eye sockets situated at top of head

skull large in proportion to body

nasal cavity situated on top of head

inner pair of incisors tusklike

deep lower jaw for muscle attachment

GIANTS OF THE WATER

A HEAVYWEIGHT OF THE AFRICAN LAKES AND RIVERS, THE HIPPO IS SOMETHING OF A JEKYLL AND HYDE: PLACID BY NIGHT, IT MAY TURN VERY NASTY INDEED BY DAY IN ITS WATERY WALLOWING GROUNDS

The word *hippopotamus*, meaning "river horse," may be misleading in regard to horses, but it aptly sums up the hippo's close relationship with water—for rivers, lakes, and wallows are central to its lifestyle. Hippos luxuriate in water; they will spend the entire day immersed, with only their eyes, nostrils, and ears breaking the surface.

On a really hot day, a hippo will sink gently out of view, to propel gracefully along the riverbed for up to five minutes at a time. A hippo manages this feat by virtue of its long, supple back and a technique of kicking with its hind limbs against the riverbed. Furthermore, hippos do not float, even with lungs filled. Emerging from a dive, the hippo exhales explosively, then recharges its lungs.

However, this aquatic lounging is far more than mere self-indulgence; the hippo depends on water in its habitat for two sound reasons. First, there is a surprisingly thin epidermis (outer skin) upon its thick, tough hide. When the hippo is out of water, this epidermis acts like a wick, and water evaporates very rapidly from its body. Without regular moisturizing, the animal would dehydrate, although its skin is preserved to some extent by the sticky pink fluid it secretes. In addition, the hippo's legs cannot support its phenomenal body weight for prolonged stretches; it likes to take the weight off its feet, and deep, open water provides the perfect medium for weightless inactivity.

THE RIVER BUS

A baby hippo often hitches a ride through the water on its mother's back, but this mode of transportation is also exploited by some unlikely species. Cattle egrets and cormorants settle on the hippo, using the platform as a midwater vantage point from which to spot a meal. After a hippo fight the birds also pick insects from the wounds; this helps

to keep the gashes free of infection. Oxpeckers perch on exposed parts of the hippo's body, nipping parasitic ticks from its skin and ridding the hippo of an itchy problem. Terrapins, too, hitch rides, often in such numbers that they virtually obscure the tolerant giant from view.

JAWING

A hippo's tolerance of other species at the watering place does not, however, extend so readily to its own kind. The restful harmony of a dozen dozing adults may be shattered in an instant by two bickering bulls—usually in the form of a jawing bout.

By the age of seven or so, bull hippos have already learned to "jaw" as a means of establishing superiority. Standing face-to-face, often

Relying for the most part on the forest canopy to keep it cool, the pygmy hippo (above) *enjoys a dip.*

Anthony Bannister/NHPA

Jonathan Scott/Planet Earth Pictures

When the day heats up, the hippos return, single file, from their feeding grounds to the water.

shoulder-deep in the water, they open their jaws wide to show off the curving canines in their lower jaws. These yawnlike gestures may develop into a fencing match, with the adversaries lunging together and ramming jaws. The show of strength is highly ritualized and usually ends in one animal backing away in defeat, receiving a slash to the rump as it retreats from the victor. But where two bulls are closely matched, neither may flee—and the consequences are sometimes fatal. By complete contrast, nighttime feeding is a peaceful affair. The hippos ignore each other, and the lush grasslands are treated as fair game.

BUSH BABY

The pygmy hippo, being largely solitary, rarely needs to fight. It has few natural enemies, and when it feels threatened, it will instinctively flee into the deepest forest undergrowth. Like its larger relative, the pygmy hippo lies low during the day. Only at nightfall does it slip out of hiding to sniff its way to a source of food, helped along its way by the dung heaps marking its forest runways. ■

KEY FACTS

● Every ten minutes, a hippo exposed to the air loses about 12 mg of water from each 0.8 sq in (5 sq cm) area of skin. This is up to five times the rate at which a human would evaporate water.

● Hippos usually restrict their grazing to within 2 miles (3 km). But if they can find waterholes farther inland, they may use these refreshing stopovers and push on for more than 6 miles (10 km) from their lake or river base.

● Nine out of every ten hippos suffer from eye troubles caused by a parasitic fluke. There are usually about eight, but up to forty, flukes attached to each hippo.

● By standing on the riverbed on its hind legs, a hippo can stretch its nose to the surface in water as deep as 19 ft (6 m).

● For all their secrecy, pygmy hippos may betray their presence when feeding: Munching on fruit or leaves, they can be heard at distances of up to 160 ft (50 m).

HABITATS

Up until two centuries ago, hippos existed in suitable habitats throughout Africa from the Nile delta south to the Cape. Their one essential requirement being water, they have never inhabited the Namib Desert of southern Africa. There is some evidence, however, that populations once existed in the central Sahara and on the Moroccan coast.

Nowadays their range has contracted, and from a once-solid distribution they have been parceled up into thousands of isolated populations. There are virtually no hippos left in north Africa, or south of the Zambezi in southern Africa. Their distribution in West Africa is reduced, although a number of healthy populations exist in Guinea, Togo, and Benin.

Pygmy hippos have probably never been widespread, dependent as they are upon equatorial rain forests. Their stronghold is Liberia, but there are also fragmented populations in Guinea, Ivory Coast, Sierra Leone, and, possibly, Nigeria and Guinea Bissau. In the case of both species, geographical distribution is very difficult to determine: Hippos move around a great deal, and pygmy hippos hide in the forests.

Richard Packwood/Oxford Scientific Films

HIPPOS ARE FOUND IN GREATEST DENSITY ALONG WINDING STRETCHES OF SMOOTH-FLOWING RIVERS WITH DEEP POOLS

An ideal habitat features rivers or lakes with firm, shelving borders, where hippos can kneel or stand in near-complete immersion. Gently sloping riverbanks also enable baby hippos to suckle in comfort. Fertile grazing pastures, or "hippo lawns," should be within easy strolling distance of the water. They like to wallow in company during the day; this requires space, and they therefore avoid thickly forested banks or stands of dense, high reeds, where space is limited. They will, however, resort more frequently to thickets in areas where they are disturbed excessively by humans.

Hippos are found at altitudes of up to 6,560 ft (2,000 m), and even on seacoasts. Populations also exist on two islands, Mafia and Zanzibar. Hippos do not, however, enjoy excessively cold water.

Where they exist along rivers, it seems that hippos have distinct habitat preferences according to the group density. From a study of a section of the Nile, it was discovered that larger hippo

David Keith Jones/Images of Africa Photobank

A heavily worn trail made by hippos on their nightly travels to their feeding lawns.

FOOD FOR FISH

Because hippos graze from the land and return to the water, they excrete a fair amount of waste into the rivers and lakes. In the process they gradually transfer nutrients into the water. The waterways and aquatic plants are so enriched by the natural fertilizer that resident fish, such as tilapia and Nile perch, enjoy a feeding bonanza. This is much to the delight of local fisheries, since, in addition, the hippo groups at the shores tend to deter the more opportunistic fishermen from exploiting the fish species' shallow-water breeding grounds.

But the association also runs in reverse. A cyprinid species of fish, *Labeo velifer*, is known to nibble upon the hides of wallowing hippos, removing caked mud and scraps of vegetation. The fish receives a meal, and, in return, the hippo's skin is cleaned and conditioned. Out of the water, birds perform the same service for the hippo groups.

A large group of hippos cooling off in the Mara River in the Masai Mara Reserve.

herds, containing two to five dozen animals, preferred the relatively shallow spits of land around estuaries, while solitary males and small groups of a dozen or so individuals were scattered somewhat at random along the banks.

FOOTPRINTS IN THE SAND

Hippos leave fairly obvious evidence of their presence by a river or lake, churning the sandy or silted banks into a marsh of mud. On their evening forays to the grazing lawns, they use regular routes up the bank and over the floodplains. These are soon worn down into twin ruts by the heavy foot traffic and are flagged at intervals by the animals' dung. These strong-smelling heaps seem to function as route markers for nighttime navigation, as well as reminders of a territorial bull's presence in the area. However, neither the paths nor the dung can be regarded as boundaries of a territory.

Territories, held only by high-ranking bulls, are usually pear-shaped, with the narrower end of the pear extending some way into the water. They can extend along the shoreline, from around 160–190 ft (50–60 m) to 800–1,600 ft (250–500 m), but they rarely penetrate further than six miles (10 km)

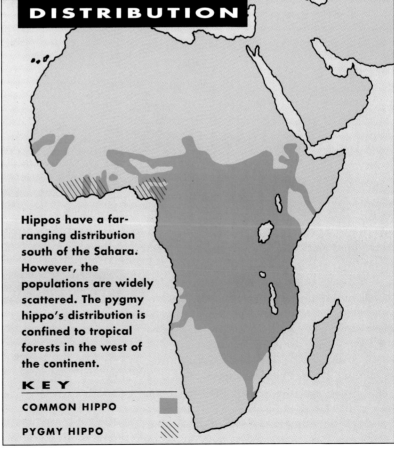

DISTRIBUTION

Hippos have a far-ranging distribution south of the Sahara. However, the populations are widely scattered. The pygmy hippo's distribution is confined to tropical forests in the west of the continent.

KEY

COMMON HIPPO

PYGMY HIPPO

inland: Water, after all, is the hippo's refuge in times of trouble. A bull may be ousted rapidly from his patch by an ambitious male, or he may hold it for several years, depending upon his fighting prowess.

The size of a male's territory depends largely on the density of the local hippo population, which itself varies constantly, according to climatic conditions and food supplies. When hippos were more abundant, one might easily have counted some 100 animals per mile (60 per kilometer). Nowadays, that number is usually a dozen or so, although groups of up to a hundred can occasionally be seen.

After a long period of hippo occupation, the bankside pastures are stripped of their grasses. Having naturally unstable groups, hippos tend to disperse—particularly during the wet season, when the widespread availability of food enables them to wander at will. As a result, the animals usually move on before they have eaten themselves into starvation. But these nomads do not leave a wasteland behind: The intense grazing clears the way for shrubs and thickets, which attract browsing mammals. At any one time, hippos may be found feeding alongside water buffalo, zebra, waterbuck, elephant, rhino, and many other savanna residents, not to mention the birds, fish, and crocodiles that benefit in various ways from the presence of hippos.

Alan Root/Survival Anglia

FOCUS ON

LAKES EDWARD AND GEORGE

The Ruwenzori, or Queen Elizabeth National Park, occupies 792 sq miles (1,980 sq km) of Uganda in the Rift Valley and is home to some of the richest, most diverse wildlife in all of Africa. The terrain is dominated by bush thickets, rich grasslands, savanna, tropical forest, and swamp, but it also includes the immense Lake Edward and much smaller Lake George. These bodies of water are linked by the 20-mile (32-km) Kazinga Channel, and between them they play host to probably 2,000 hippos—around one-third of Uganda's total complement. Indeed, some of the most detailed studies of hippos—their lifestyle and the ways in which they affect local ecosystems—have been conducted around Lake Edward and Lake George.

TEMPERATURE AND RAINFALL

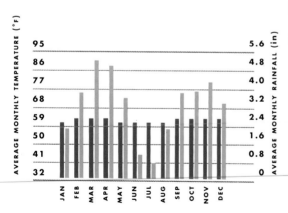

■ **TEMPERATURE**

■ **RAINFALL**

The chart shows temperatures and rainfall for Kubali. Temperature is constant throughout the year at 61–63°F. Rainfall varies between 1 and 5 in, but one can almost set a watch by the time it rains— 5:00–6:00 P.M. daily.

The pygmy hippo, too, is dependent on water, and its favorite habitat is a dense stand of forest containing plenty of streams or swampy patches. Here, each hippo occupies a home range. Bulls roam more widely than cows, and their ranges may encroach upon those of a number of cows. Within its home range, each individual wanders along set paths. These appear as beaten tracks in areas of thin ground cover and as leafy green tunnels in denser growth. These trails are marked, like those of the larger hippo, by scattered heaps of dung. ■

NEIGHBORS

Uganda is a prime stopover point for migrants, and over 500 species have been seen in Ruwenzori. The lions of the park are unusual in that they frequently climb trees to escape flying insects.

CARP

Introduced to Africa by European settlers, the carp has become one of its most common freshwater fish.

OXPECKER

This bird lives up to its name by perching on grazing mammals to peck parasites from their hides.

Neighbor illustrations Joanne Cowne/Oxpecker by Elisabeth Smith

RUWENZORI

The Ruwenzori National Park lies in the extreme southwest of Uganda, close to the Zaire border. It is flanked by the Ruwenzori mountains in the west and Lake Victoria in the east. To its north, Lake Albert is fed by the Albert Nile, the southernmost stretch of the mighty White Nile.

TERRAPIN

Sometimes scores of river terrapins are seen on a hippo's back, where they bask in the sun.

NILE CROCODILE

This deadly predator lurks in African waterways, waiting for unsuspecting mammals to drink.

HAMMERKOP

This large wader is active mainly at night. It stirs up mud on the river bottom to get to its prey.

THOMSON'S GAZELLE

Slight of frame and elegant in profile, the "Tommy" is one of the savanna's fastest-running residents.

AFRICAN WILD DOG

Also called the Cape hunting dog, this animal lives in strong family groups and hunts in packs.

SOCIAL STRUCTURE

The sight of hippos wallowing indolently in the cooling, muddy shallows, casually wagging their ears in the hazy heat, belies the fact that their social structure is founded throughout upon brute force and bloody confrontation. For sheer bullying pugnacity, the territorial bulls reign supreme, yet even they must fawn submissively when selecting a potential mate from among a herd of cows.

The best that can be said is that they do form associations and establish temporary pecking orders among both bulls and cows, particularly in densely packed populations where living space is at a premium. Social ties are correspondingly looser in larger stretches of prime habitat where hippos lie thinner on the ground; in such relaxed conditions, too, fights are less frequent.

COWS AND BULLS

The firmest bond among hippos is that between a mother and her calf, whom she has taught from its earliest days to stick by her side. This bond may last for many years, as cows can be seen leading a file of young of various generations; these trot obediently behind her—the baby in her wake, the eldest forming the rearguard. The cow may even "baby-sit" nonrelated subadults. When threatened, cows and young cluster in the water to protect the tiniest calves or each other, giving rise to female-led or matriarchal herds.

A bull rises through the ranks by sheer aggres-

HIPPO GROUPS

Groups of any size may combine in every possible permutation (above). *However, nonbreeding males usually bunch together in unstable bachelor parties* (top right).

BULLFIGHTERS

Senior bulls battle for territorial control (left). *These fearsome fights are watched by the whole group, which join in with the battle cries. The fights sometimes end in death.*

Illustrations John Cox/Wildlife Art Agency

sion, and having fought his way to the top, wins control of a prime territory. He usually achieves this at the age of twenty years or more. Females are attracted to the comfort of these "luxury areas," but a bull is unlikely to retain control of more than one or two of them for long.

TALKING AT BOTH ENDS

A bull hippo's social etiquette involves making a show of strength in highly dramatic but strictly ritualized ceremonies. He defecates in spectacular fashion, whirring and waggling his stubby tail to spatter semiliquid dung in a wide shower at special points on his territory and feeding trails. The pungent heaps of dung are a rich information source for all individuals, telling them who is boss. Territorial bulls also defecate over cows and juveniles, on land or in the water. In turn, wallowing cows and young turn away from the bull, cower in submission, and wag their tails, urinating and splashing river water. This allows the bull to sample a cow's urine, to assess her sexual condition.

At frequent intervals, territorial bulls meet at their boundaries to engage in the highly ritualized voiding of waste. More aggressive confrontations take place in the water.

By comparison, pygmy hippo confrontations are low-key affairs. Like hippos, they tail-wag to spread dung, and probably use these middens to flag their presence in order to avoid each other. ■

ⓘⓃ SIGHT

WIDENING WEAPONS

A bull hippo's jaw armament is vital to his status and, quite possibly, survival. Defecation rituals may settle the finer points of superiority, but when push comes to shove, it is the language of razor-sharp canines that wins territory, mating opportunities, and the right to live. Some studies suggest that the hippo's reliance on jaw-power has its roots in the species' earliest development stages.

Jonathan Scott/Planet Earth Pictures

FOOD AND FEEDING

The hippo is a grazer, feeding on the grasslands adjoining its resting places on the river. It concentrates on lush, shallow-rooted grasses, as well as nutritious creeping varieties. These form the mainstay of its diet, although it may scoop up plants such as duckweed, and it has even been known to browse on the bark, foliage, and fruit of trees.

Usually at dusk, hippos rouse themselves from the water and head purposefully for the riverside feeding grounds. In areas with human disturbance, they may not make the expedition until well into the night—and then only if clouds cover the moon. By contrast, hippos in more trouble-free areas may graze in the late afternoon and early morning. Although feeding activities are fairly synchronized, hippos do not graze as a social group but scatter. The exception to this rule is a female with her youngster.

In times of plenty, when fresh, rain-fed grazing is plentiful, hippos can forage almost at the water's edge. Drier periods oblige them to travel two miles (three kilometers) or more over land to find sufficiently green pastures; at such times, the rutted trails marked by prominent dunghills help them find their way in the darkness. Once hippos reach their chosen feeding grounds, they set to work with a will—the less time spent out of the supportive river water, the better. Occasionally, individuals trek back to the river to take a rest.

The canines and incisors are not used in grazing; instead, the hippo uses its immensely broad, horny lips to grasp and crop the grasses, using the natural swing of its heavy head to tear up the sward. The whiskery hairs on its muzzle help it to assess the length and nature of the grass. It is then left to the molars to grind up the fodder to a coarse mash.

The hippos' heavy breathing and steady chomping carry far through the African night air. Within five hours or so, each hippo has had its fill and

FEEDING LAWNS

Hippos travel along well-worn paths to their main feeding areas, or "hippo lawns." They also eat aquatic plants at their daytime resting places.

returns to the river to sleep. If the grazing has been good, the hippo may well return to the same patch the following evening.

The fodder is digested chiefly in the upper three sections of the stomach. The hippo does not chew its food a second time, as ruminants do, but its digestion works in a similar fashion, if a little more slowly: It has a particularly long intestine, and the fermenting processes in its stomach get to work at around midday following a nightly feed.

A herd of grazing hippos can have a marked effect upon the grassland: Weak-rooted grasses are quickly eradicated, while tougher clumps are left behind. This would seem to spell trouble for the hippos' hungry neighboring grazers—buffalo, antelope, and others—but often the opposite is true: Shrubby plants are given more freedom to spread over a riverside lawn that has been heavily

HALFWAY HOMES

If there are any muddy wallows along the way, hippos will often pause to lie in them for a while. These rest stops enable the hippos to travel farther each night in search of food.

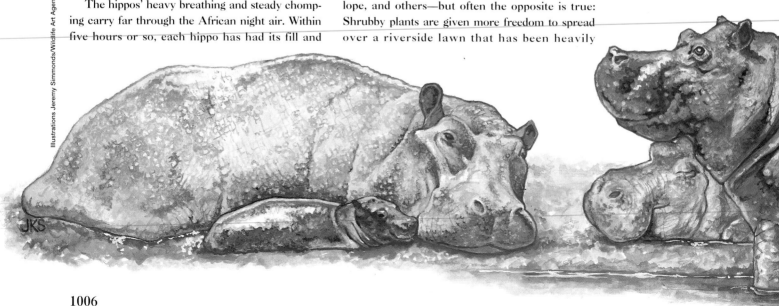

"mowed" by hippos, and these shrubs provide extra browsing for the animals of the savanna. Ultimately hippos can—and often do—eat themselves out of house and home, particularly around 1.5–2 miles (2–3 km) of the riverbank.

FOREST BROWSER

The pygmy hippo has an altogether different diet, taking advantage of the wide range of foodstuffs in its rain forest home. Like its large cousin, it crops grasses, but its narrower muzzle enables it to browse selectively on other foodstuff. It plucks the fresh foliage of saplings, bushes, herbs, and ferns and eats the fallen fruit from the tropical jungle floor. Unlike the hippo, the pygmy hippo often uses its canine teeth. It rips up aquatic plants by the roots, devouring any tubers that it exposes, and crunches up fibrous fruits. Once it has stripped the foliage from the lower branches of a favorite tree, it may even rear on its hind legs and walk as far as its forelegs will reach up, so as to reach the higher growth. ■

Mark Hamblin/Oxford Scientific Films

EATING LITTLE

Surprisingly for such a colossal animal, the hippo eats remarkably little. The difficulty in observing its nighttime activities makes information rather sketchy, and estimates of its daily food requirements vary vastly from 25 to 150 kg (55 to 330 lb). It appears, however, that a hippo eats only around 1–1.5 percent of its body weight in food each day; by comparison, the figure for cattle and many other ruminants is closer to 2.5 percent. The hippo does not need to eat more: It burns up very little energy in seeking out food and is accomplished at doing practically nothing during daylight hours. Indeed, when necessary, hippos may spend several weeks without eating, surviving probably on fat reserves previously accumulated in nighttime forages.

LIFE CYCLE

For the hippo, breeding begins in the dry season so that births occur during the wet season, when food will be abundant for lactating mothers.

If an adult bull does not already have control of a receptive female, he must go out and select one— and in his quest for a mate, he exhibits a rare submissiveness. He approaches a herd of females to seek out a sexually receptive mate, but if any female rises to her feet, he hastily cowers to the ground and defecates as a gesture of submission. Once she has settled down again, he works his way quietly through the crowd, dropping to his haunches at the smallest sign of female irritability.

When he finally finds a female in estrus, it is his turn to assert authority again. Chasing her into the shallows, he subdues and mounts her, punctuating his efforts with loud wheeze-honks. When his mate raises her head from the water to breathe or tries to break away from his hold, he responds by snapping his jaws at her until, the coupling accomplished, he releases her from his immense weight.

At 32–37 weeks, gestation is short for such a massive mammal. As a female nears her birthing time, her aggression mounts. She leaves her group shortly before giving birth, seeking the seclusion of reed beds some distance away. She gives birth either in shallow water or on dry land.

Slipping hind-first into the world, the calf is far from helpless. Within a few minutes it can walk and also suckle underwater; however, it can hold its breath

for little more than 30 seconds at this stage.

Precocious it may be, but the newborn is still highly vulnerable, measuring only 3 ft (91 cm) long and weighing a paltry 60 lb (27 kg). Adult males are no less a threat than lions or hyenas, and the female guards her young determinedly. The pair stays away from the herd for up to two weeks, during which period the calf suckles regularly. After this, it takes its place in a female-led nursery, where it receives a greater level of protection. Here it enjoys the company of other young hippos, with whom it wrestles and jaws in play.

Although its mother lactates for a year or so, the youngster first receives grass at around a month old, and, within five months of birth, is visiting the pastures to graze. The first year of life is the most dangerous: Some 45 percent of youngsters do not survive it. If a bull hippo makes it to sexual maturity, at 3–4 years of age, his search for a mate may drive him into deadly conflict with other, more senior bulls.

BONDING

The calf soon learns to recognize its mother and never strays far from her side. It frequently rides piggyback when she enters deeper waters. The mother and young rejoin the rest of the group after a week or two.

Nestling against its mother in the water (right), a young calf has her complete protection. When feeding underwater, it breaks away regularly to gasp for air.

MATING

Hippos mate either in water or on land. The cow lowers her body to encourage the bull, who then holds her down with his body weight.

Illustrations Evi Antoniou

L. Lee Rue/FLPA

GROWING UP

The life of a young hippo

BRINGING UP BABY

The female hippo must bring up her calf without the help of her jealous mate, who may try to drive away and even kill the youngster. For its first few weeks, the calf looks upon its mother as a source of milk, protection, and education.

The newborn calf, however, has no idea who its mother is. Given the chance, it is just as likely to trot toward any other large moving object, such as a buffalo or even a human. So it must imprint upon, or learn to recognize, its mother. The pair's virtual isolation from the group helps in this respect, and within a couple of weeks each recognizes the other.

Cows reach sexual maturity at 3–4 years old; they too must learn to stand their ground in a life that is seldom free from aggression or outright violence.

PYGMY HIPPOS

Pygmy hippos may breed at any time in their rain forest home, but mating probably peaks in the dry season. A bull tracks down a cow in estros probably by sniffing out her dung piles. As a rule, cows give birth to a single calf every other year.

Gestation lasts 25–30 weeks. The pygmy hippo cow does not give birth in water, but she makes sure that the calf's sensitive skin is kept moist to prevent inflammation. She sets up her newborn in concealing vegetation by a forest stream, returning to nurse and suckle it about three times each day.

The calf suckles for several months, putting on about a pound (0.5 kg) each day, and at about three months old is ready to take solid food. It stays with its mother for about three years. When sexually mature, the young hippo must make its own way in life, in a new part of the forest. ∎

BIRTH

When the calf is born in water, its mother supports it so it can breathe. Sometimes birth takes place on land or in shallow water.

SUCKLING

The calf suckles a few times each day, holding the nipple with the surface of its tongue. It can even suckle underwater.

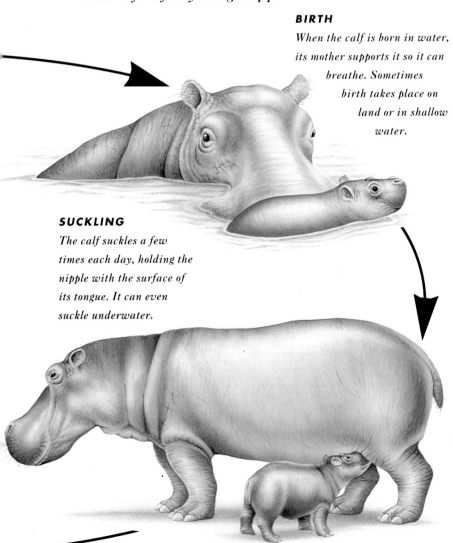

FROM BIRTH TO DEATH

HIPPOPOTAMUS	PYGMY HIPPOPOTAMUS
GESTATION: 32–37 WEEKS	**GESTATION:** 25–30 WEEKS
NO. OF YOUNG: 1, VERY RARELY 2	**NO. OF YOUNG:** 1
WEIGHT AT BIRTH: 75–120 LB (35–55 KG)	**WEIGHT AT BIRTH:** 10-15 LB (4.5–7 KG)
FIRST WALKING: WITHIN MINUTES	**FIRST WALKING:** WITHIN MINUTES
WEANING: 6–8 MONTHS	**WEANING:** 6–8 MONTHS
SEXUAL MATURITY/BULL: 3–4 YEARS	**SEXUAL MATURITY/BULL:** 3–5 YEARS
SEXUAL MATURITY/FEMALE: 3–4 YEARS (BUT 4–5 YEARS IN CAPTIVITY)	**SEXUAL MATURITY/FEMALE:** 3–5 YEARS
LIFE SPAN: 40–50 YEARS	**LIFE SPAN:** UP TO 42 YEARS

GIANT IN DECLINE

ALTHOUGH PROTECTED THROUGHOUT MUCH OF ITS RANGE, THE LARGE, LUMBERING HIPPO FREQUENTLY FINDS ITSELF IN CONFLICT WITH ITS HUMAN NEIGHBORS, AND CASUALTIES CAN BE HIGH ON BOTH SIDES

A s a species, the hippo is overall in fairly good shape—compared to, for example, its neighbors the rhinos and elephants. But a recent investigation conducted by the International Union for the Conservation of Nature (IUCN) has concluded that the species' status is experiencing disturbing downward trends. The IUCN requested full reports from each country in Africa and compiled what is currently the most thorough and up-to-date status survey on both species of hippopotamuses. The IUCN's very rough estimate for the common hippo's total wild population stands at 157,000, the bulk of which exists in southern and eastern Africa.

WHERE ARE THEY NOW?

The hippo's southern African stronghold is in Zambia, where there are probably 40,000 individuals. Some 20–25,000 of these live in the Luangwa Valley. Malawi holds some 10,000 hippos, particularly on the various Shire river systems and Lake Malawi. The Zambezi river, in Mozambique and Zimbabwe, is another vital refuge. In the Republic of South Africa itself, the greatest numbers are to be found in Kruger National Park, where legal protection is also well enforced. There are currently no figures available for Angola, owing to the country's political problems, but hippos were once numerous in this country. The approximate total of hippos in southern Africa is 80,000 individuals.

Roughly 70,000 live in eastern Africa. Here, the southern reaches of the Nile (the White and Albert Niles) and its many tributaries are well stocked with hippos. Tanzania's sumptuous Selous reserve is home to some 17,000; Zaire holds around 30,000; and populations in Ethiopia, Tanzania, Uganda, and the Sudan make up the eastern African total. But there were once many more. In Queen Elizabeth Park, for example, hippo numbers soared to some 21,000 before the 1950s, but a controversial culling program around Lakes Edward and George in the late 1950s reduced the park's population to 14,000. In the troubled Idi Amin years of the 1970s, poaching became rife and numbers were slashed to a mere 2,000—roughly the population there today. Nevertheless, eastern Africa as a whole remains a significant refuge for hippos.

The hippo's real problems lie in West Africa, where the species is now severely fragmented into several isolated populations—some of which comprise fewer than 50 individuals. Equatorial Guinea, Guinea Bissau, and Senegal hold the greatest numbers, with smaller populations surviving in Burkina Faso, Gambia, Sierra Leone, and other countries. In total, there are perhaps 7,000 hippos in West Africa.

Clearly, it is impossible to obtain precise population figures, since hippos migrate here and there

Overgrazing by hippos causes extensive damage to land, mainly through soil erosion (above).

Anthony Bannister/NHPA

Stephen Dalton/NHPA

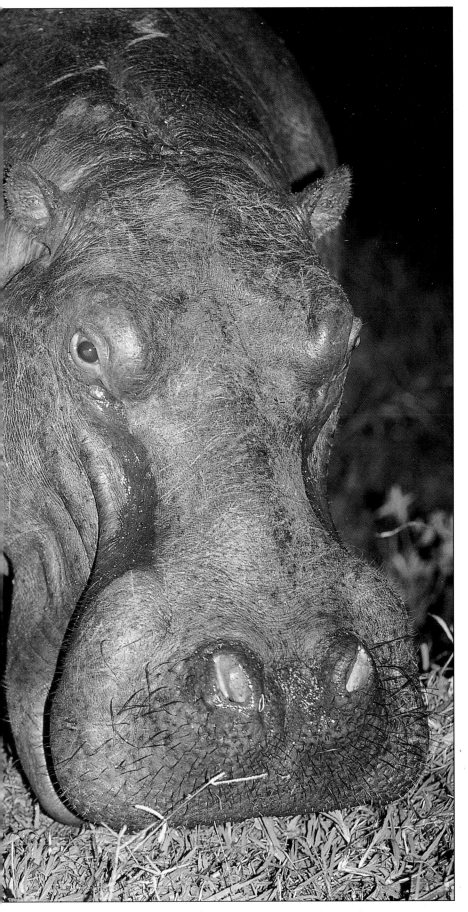

This map shows the former and present distribution of the common hippopotamus.

FORMER   PRESENT

The hippo was once common over much of sub-Saharan Africa, wherever grazing and water were in sufficient supply. It also existed along the Nile in Egypt, as far as the river's delta. Although its numbers have been declining gradually for hundreds of years, it still maintained much of its original range until the late 1950s.

Today the hippo's range has receded from Egypt in the north and from South Africa in the south. Its populations in West Africa have been hard hit and are now fragmented into small, isolated populations.

across national boundaries. Also, they spend their daylight hours in water and cannot accurately be counted by aerial survey.

In 14 out of 34 African countries, downward trends in hippo populations have been reported, with declines also suspected in a further 4. In 5 countries the situation is said to be stable; population increases have been noted in only 2 countries. Only 11 countries described their hippos as widespread, and 1 country alone—Zaire— reported hippos occurring at high densities.

The hippo is assured total legal protection in 22 out of 34 countries, but only 9 of these 22 could claim that the protection was effectively enforced.

A hippo grazes in Kruger National Park, South Africa, where protection is well enforced.

ENDANGERED SPECIES

Stephen Dalton/NHPA

CULLING CONTROVERSY

Although each hippo eats relatively little in proportion to its body size, there is no denying that an entire grazing group can rapidly strip grassland to a critical level, leaving land barren. Such a situation occurred in Uganda's Queen Elizabeth Park, which was established in 1952. Hippo populations escalated to such a density that they seriously overgrazed the land, cutting deep gulleys in the banks and stripping the grass and scrub.

In a bid to protect the land, the Uganda National Parks Trustees made the unprecedented decision in 1957 to set up a culling program combined with a hippo management project from 1962 to 1966, with the aim of controlling hippo groups at sustainable densities. By the mid-1960s, the measures had proven successful and other grazing mammals were able to return to the lakeshores. But success was short-lived. After management operations ceased in 1967 and political upheaval struck Uganda during the 1970s, the problems returned in full. Culling and control still remain controversial issues.

Civil unrest is partly to blame in countries such as Angola, Mozambique, and Rwanda. Protective legislation is also ignored by local villagers because they have their own plans for land use—many of Africa's national parks and reserves have admittedly been established without full consideration of the needs and wants of local people.

WHY THE DECLINE?

Much of Africa is prone to cycles of drought. The hippo, being dependent on water, obviously suffers during particularly dry periods—especially where its groups are densely packed into limited suitable habitat. The general desertification of Mali in West Africa, for example, is causing problems for its resident hippos.

Overall, far more serious than drought is the loss of grazing. Timber industries and fisheries are expanding in Equatorial Guinea, and large-scale irrigation projects are under way in Zimbabwe; all of these commercial ventures threaten prime grazing habitat. Furthermore, the lush grasslands beside rivers and lakes are perfect for hippos, but they are also ripe for farming—and the loss of grazing habitat to agriculture is the most significant threat to the hippo throughout Africa.

THE PYGMY HIPPO

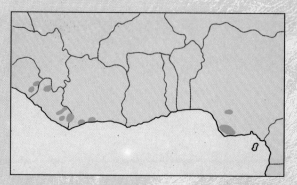

The pygmy hippo is an example of a species that has been projected straight from near-total obscurity into suspected extreme rarity. Almost all the current knowledge of its lifestyle and distribution has been gleaned from sightings within the last decade—and these sightings have been very rare indeed. Conservationists can therefore only assume that it is in trouble, and the species is currently listed by the IUCN as vulnerable.

As a species confined to tropical forests, the pygmy hippo is at risk from any level of forest clearance. In its Liberian stronghold, deforestation is rife and looks set to remain that way, since there are few effective controls on such land alteration. Unfortunately, Liberia has suffered from recent political upheaval. And, as a result, the species' conservation is receiving low priority. The one relatively secure site for the pygmy hippo is Liberia's Sapo National Park, where it is known to live and where protection is strongly enforced.

CONSERVATION MEASURES

● The pygmy hippo is listed on Appendix II by CITES (The Convention on International Trade in Endangered Species). This appendix imposes legally enforceable restrictions on any species considered at risk of becoming endangered.

● Full legal protection has been conferred upon the pygmy hippo in all countries in which it is known to occur.

The pygmy hippo is also hunted for its flesh in all countries except equatorial Guinea and is apparently hunted for its teeth in Liberia. It is persecuted by people in Sierra Leone, due to its unfortunate habit of trampling over gardens and plantations on the vicinity of its moist, forested home. While these factors also affect the larger hippo, they are much more of a threat to the pygmy hippo simply because it exists throughout its range in such critically low numbers. The combined effects of habitat loss, hunting, and persecution serve only to fragment the remaining pygmy hippo populations, making it ever more difficult for the species to breed successfully.

HIPPOS IN DANGER

THE INTERNATIONAL UNION FOR THE CONSERVATION OF NATURE (IUCN), OR THE WORLD CONSERVATION UNION, LISTS THE FOLLOWING SPECIES OR SUBSPECIES OF HIPPOPOTAMUS:

PYGMY HIPPO	VULNERABLE
NIGERIAN PYGMY HIPPO	INDETERMINATE

IT MUST BE NOTED, HOWEVER, THAT SINCE THE NIGERIAN PYGMY HIPPO HAS NOT BEEN SEEN IN ABOUT FIFTY YEARS, THE STATUS OF THIS SUBSPECIES MAY PERHAPS BE MORE REALISTICALLY CLASSED AS ENDANGERED OR EVEN EXTINCT.

Inset Rafi Ben-Shahar/Oxford Scientific Films

THE RARELY SIGHTED PYGMY HIPPO (*ABOVE*). THE FUTURE OF THIS SPECIES IS NOW UNDER THREAT.

● The pygmy hippo is further protected in Liberia by The Wildlife and National Park Act of 1988. There is, however, little evidence that the legislation is enforced except in Sapo National Park.

● Pygmy hippos are being bred in captivity in many collections worldwide. Stud book listings enable zoos to exchange animals and sustain a healthy gene pool.

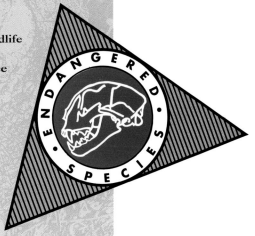

When farmers parcel up the hippo's former grazing lawns, its populations become isolated and small in number. Small populations breed less efficiently since their genetic diversity is reduced. Hippos normally achieve a healthy mix of genes by the natural instability of their groups: a few individuals break away to another group to find mates, and the risk of inbreeding is lessened. This free living is obviously impossible where crop fields pin groups down in restricted habitats. To make matters worse, agricultural development leads to conflict between hippos and local people.

THE KILLING FIELDS

In Gambia, farmers have been growing rice for more than 250 years. With a rising human population, rice cultivation has escalated—and the common hippos love it. They crop the tender tips of the rice shoots, damaging the harvest. In a number of instances the government was called in to investigate: It concluded that, although the farmers' claims were exaggerated, control measures were in order. Hunters were brought in to gun down the hippos, whose carcasses provided sumptuous feasts for the local inhabitants. Independent observers noted, however, that the grazed rice crops hardly suffered at all, and grew back in a matter of days.

The story is similar in other African countries; hippos both graze and trample crops, in many cases wreaking havoc on harvests. Indeed, it is said that a single hippo can ruin a farmer's entire yearly crop in one night. More worrisome, the animals present a very real threat to human life. When fishermen steer their boats toward a hippo group, the hippos naturally resent the intrusion, often overturning or crushing boats in the general commotion and causing fishermen to drown. There is some evidence

ALONGSIDE MAN

HUBERT THE TRAVELING HIPPO

Being naturally sedentary creatures, hippos rarely travel farther than they have to, although a lack of food may drive them 25 miles (40 km) or more to find fresh sustenance. But once in a while, hippos make a trek of epic proportions. A famous account tells how one hippo, which came to be known as "Hubert," set off from Zululand in 1928 and meandered alone over Natal and Cape Province—apparently out of idle curiosity.

Hubert made regular pit stops at water holes and riverbanks, to the delight of local newspaper reporters. He even passed through the city of Durban, where he astonished residents by investigating open doorways and school yards. By the time he had covered some 400 miles (644 km), Hubert had won South Africa's heart and had even been given full legal protection.

But Hubert's trampling feet won little respect from farmers. And, sadly, in April 1930, an angry crop grower shot him dead. It was only then, following the investigation into the unfortunate incident, that the truth came to light: Hubert was in fact Huberta—a female hippo.

that hippos charge people, but this may be the result of deliberate provocation—or of people committing the extreme folly of standing between a nervous hippo and its river refuge. Whatever the true cause of each fatal confrontation, it is generally acknowledged that hippos engender more human deaths than do any other African animal—lions and snakes included.

Considering the hippo's capacity for destruction, its persecution at the hands of humans can be understood—if not wholly justified. One solution to the problem is to erect fencing around crop fields and the outlying parts of villages. It is surprisingly easy to set up effective barriers, since hippos do not like stepping over any kind of obstacle. Indeed, even when charging in panic at a human in their path, they often draw up at the last moment and swerve harmlessly to one side. Trials in the field show that fences no higher than 3 ft (1 m) will deter a curious hippo. However, any large-scale plan to fence off rice paddies would probably have to be executed using wire fences, since the use of timber would mean felling precious savanna woodlands. In fact, low wire fences work perfectly well, especially when electrified and festooned with tin cans.

FORBIDDEN FLESH

The hippo suffers surprisingly little from hunting for its meat; the flesh is said to be tasty and is certainly widely eaten. In many Muslim African communities, however, hippo meat is not consumed because of the animal's affiliation to pigs. In Zambia's Luangwa Valley, where the hippo thrives, locals refuse to eat its meat through fears of catching leprosy—a superstition that may stem from an outbreak in 1987 of the anthrax disease, that killed thousands of resident hippos. Disease is not usually a problem among hippos, although rinderpest, an infection troubling many grazing species, killed several hippos between 1929 and 1946.

A COMMERCIAL PROSPECT

Trophy hunters obtain little of interest from the hippo, other than its canines, which are carved—rather like elephant ivory—to produce trinkets and souvenirs. There is some trade in skins in Burundi, Senegal, Zaire, and a few other countries, but to no great degree. The hippo ivory trade is also minimal at the moment, although conservationists are concerned that the recent restrictions upon elephant ivory may turn ivory traders' attentions toward the hippo. Already, there are tentative plans in Tanzania to harvest the hippo for its teeth. If this particular proposal is put into action, Tanzania will probably instigate strict culling methods, but should the trade escalate uncontrollably—as was the case with the elephant—then the hippo could be in trouble. The hippo has unfortunately proven its fearsome capacity for inflicting harm on farmers and fishermen, but it presents an absurdly easy target to a gun-carrying poacher. ∎

When suitable grazing land is in short supply, the hippo may have to venture farther afield.

M. D. England/Ardea

INTO THE FUTURE

Although the hippo is under no immediate threat of becoming endangered, there is still good reason to be concerned about its smaller populations—particularly in West Africa. Many of these are considered too small to be self-sustaining. Furthermore, if the small but widespread populations actually disappear, the genetic diversity of the species as a whole will be reduced. Hippos cannot easily adapt to new environments, so it is seen as particularly important to preserve their remaining habitats. Efforts to this end will probably be concentrated in West Africa, where fragmented populations have relatively little access to suitable living space. In the pygmy hippo's case, full attention will be given to the area around Sapo National Park.

Before further action can be taken, conservationists need a lot more information on the hippo's status. Since the animals have no regard for national

PREDICTION

THE SMALLER, THE SCARCER

As a species, the hippo's future is secure in the short term, but small, isolated wild populations will soon disappear unless given immediate attention. The pygmy hippo may survive in the wild for only a few decades more unless it, too, receives effective habitat protection. If its wild populations disappear, its long-term survival in captivity is also doubtful.

borders (many of which are delineated by rivers or lakes), all the countries involved will need to conduct censuses on a fully international basis.

But it is no good trying to preserve the species if conservationists ride roughshod over the needs of local people—the hippo is a threat to their lives and livelihoods. Wherever land is earmarked for prime hippo territory, equal consideration should be given to fencing off nearby crop fields and villages. By the same token, local people may need to change their attitude toward the hippo—and nowhere more so than in Liberia. Most Liberians are probably unaware of their country's unique importance as the pygmy hippo's stronghold, but equally there is no good reason why they should rejoice about the fact; Liberia has endured political turmoil for some years. A program for educating people in the species' plight should be planned with a careful sense of timing. ∎

CAPTIVE BREEDING

There are hippos in many zoos around the world—but primarily for entertainment or for research, since the species is currently faring well enough in the wild. Hippos are easily tamed and breed readily in captivity, but nevertheless have a low birthrate. However, juvenile survival is well above that in nature. If, in the future, the species' survival should come to depend upon captive-bred populations, zoos have developed scientific propagation programs to which they could easily add the hippo.

For the pygmy hippo, the day of reckoning is probably too close for comfort. With its increasing rarity in the wild, the role of captive breeding is already important to the species' survival. There are more than 340 captive individuals in some 130 collections worldwide; this number represents an increase by more than 100 percent since 1970. Now that captive populations are established, zoos are already adding the pygmy hippo to their list of scientifically managed endangered species. Issues related to all areas of management, including the species' natural behaviors, feeding requirements, and veterinary concerns, are all addressed in the master plans. Genetic and demographic management ensures that all lineages will be preserved, and the numbers of animals are monitored so that they do not exceed the capacity of their captive habitat.

Illustration Joanne Cowne

HORSES

Together with zebras, horses and asses are called odd-toed ungulates of the order Perissodactyla. Also included in the order are the rhinos and less well-known tapirs, which are also less widely spread. Even-toed ungulates, order Artiodactyla, have an infinitely greater number of species. However, the Perissodactyla was the first of the two orders to evolve.

ORDER
Perissodactyla
(odd-toed ungulates)

FAMILY
Equidae
(horses)

GENUS
Equus

SPECIES
caballus
(domestic horse)

asinus
(African wild ass)

hemionus
(Asiatic wild ass)

kiang
(wild ass)

ONE-TOED SPEEDSTERS

HORSES AND ASSES ARE KNOWN THE WORLD OVER, PRIMARILY FOR THEIR LONG ASSOCIATION WITH HUMANS. BUT CENTURIES AGO, THESE FLEET-FOOTED GRAZERS ROAMED WILD AND FREE, UNTAMED BY MAN

Alerted by a movement on the horizon, a stallion lifts his proud head and stands motionless to view the scene. With nostrils flaring and head tossing, he whinnies to his herd of mares and foals and, rounding them up, sends them galloping across the plains, bringing up the rear himself. Fleet of foot, they will soon shake off any possible predators.

Wild horses once roamed in the thousands over much of Europe and Asia. Such herds may now be seen in parts of the United States and Australia, although the horses are not truly wild, but merely feral—descendants of domestic animals that have returned to the wild.

Today the family Equidae contains the horse, two or three species of asses, and three of zebras. Its evolution through some 55 million years has been well charted by fossil remains and is more complete than almost any other type of mammal. The first horse appeared some 60 million years ago.

Przhevalski's horse (right) *is a hardy creature, native to the Altai Mountains of Mongolia.*

Eohippus (ee-o-HIPP-us) was no bigger than a lamb, and had three toes on each hind foot and four on each forefoot. It was found in North America, western Europe, and eastern Asia.

As time passed, the limbs lengthened and toes were reduced to one digit; the dentition changed to suit a grazing rather than browsing lifestyle, and the body became larger, with a less arched spine. By the Oligocene epoch (38–25 million years ago), horses had died out in Europe and Asia; for a while, their evolution continued in North America.

BY THE LATE MIOCENE EPOCH, MANY EQUIDS HAD SPECIAL, FUSED LIMB BONES TO REDUCE INJURY WHILE GALLOPING

An example of the time was *Mesohippus* (MESS-o-HIPP-us), which was taller than *Eohippus* and had three toes on each foot. Its near-horizontal spine gave greater speed and stamina, enabling it to escape predators on the grassy plains.

In the later Miocene epoch, horses spread back to Europe and Asia over the land bridges present at the time. One Miocene equid was *Merychippus* (meh-ree-CHIP-us), from which it is said that all later horses evolved.

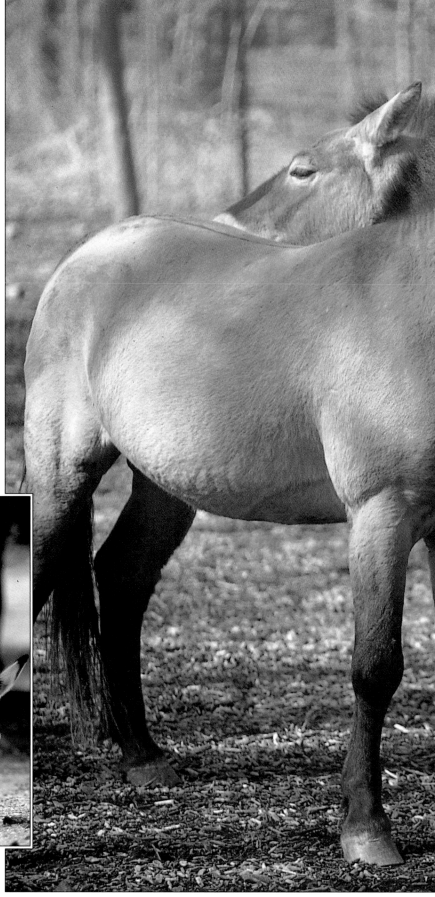

Norman Owen Tomalin/Bruce Coleman Ltd.

Mark D. Phillips/Oxford Scientific Films

The Somali wild ass (above) *is a surefooted inhabitant of the rocky wastes of Africa.*

1018

An Asiatic wild ass grazes peacefully with her foal (below) in northern Iran.

Dr. Frieder Sauer/Bruce Coleman Ltd.

The first one-toed horse, *Pliohippus* (PLY-o-HIP-us), appeared less than five million years ago. Although its remains have been found only in the United States, it was probably present also in Europe and Asia, where it gave rise to the modern horse, *Equus caballus* (ECK-wus cah-BAL-us), some time during the last million years. It colonized the steppe grasslands of Europe, Asia and Africa, but for some reason was absent from North America.

All modern breeds of horses are species, or subspecies, of *Equus caballus*. Przhevalski's horse, of the Altai Mountains in Mongolia, may be either a separate species or a subspecies of *Equus caballus*—this is

FROM THREE TOES TO ONE TOE

The earliest equids had three or four toes on each foot and walked through tropical jungles on the fleshy soles of their feet. Lacking true weapons such as claws or teeth, and being small, they hid from predators among the marshy vegetation.

But when later equids took to the open, grassy plains, they needed to run fast from their enemies. Equids developed longer legs, and the toes gave way to one digit on each foot—the hoof, which in today's horses is a hard pad. A softer V-shaped growth, called the frog, on the sole of the hoof provides a cushion to absorb shocks and pressure as the animal gallops over hard ground.

still debated by experts. Equally, opinions differ on whether the kiang is a separate species or a subspecies of the Asiatic ass.

Horses and asses are essentially long-legged animals with a harmoniously proportioned body, powerful hindquarters, a slight hump at the base of the neck, and a slight dip in the center of the back. Males are never more than 10 percent larger than females, and often less than this. The neck is long and straight, with a coarse mane along its crest. Sometimes there is a forelock— a bunch of hairs between the ears. The head is quite large, and all species have erect, mobile ears. The single hoof on each limb is supported by powerful ligaments. Horses have tails of long hairs; asses have a tuft of short hairs only at the tip of the tail.

Coat color varies, particularly in modern breeds of horses. Przhevalski's horse and asses tend to match their environment, usually a gray or sandy brown, generally with a dark stripe down the back and, sometimes, faint stripes on the lower legs.

Equids have acute hearing and excellent eyesight; they have color vision and at night can see as well as dogs and owls. ■

PRZHEVALSKI'S HORSE

Equus przewalskii
(ECK-wus psheh-VAHL-ski)

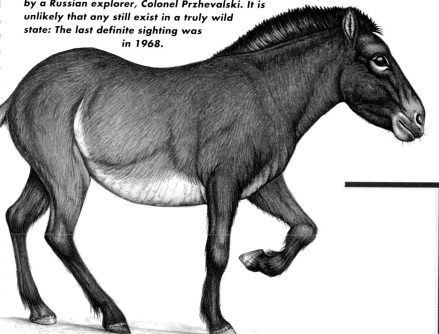

This horse is considered by some experts to be a subspecies of Equus caballus; others believe it to be a species in its own right and the ancestor of Equus caballus. Known also as the Asiatic or Mongolian wild horse, it is certainly an old species, although it was only discovered in the last century by a Russian explorer, Colonel Przhevalski. It is unlikely that any still exist in a truly wild state: The last definite sighting was in 1968.

ANCESTORS

THE DAWN HORSE
The first equid ancestor was the dawn horse or *Eohippus*, also known as *Hyracotherium*. It appeared around 60–40 million years ago and looked like a small, hornless antelope. Standing only 10–15 in (25–37 cm) at the shoulder, it had short hair, a thick neck, a small head, a stumpy tail, and thin, fine legs. Its fleshy body was longer in proportion to its neck and head, with an arched backbone. The neck carried the head at an angle suitable for browsing on low vegetation, rather than for reaching down to graze.

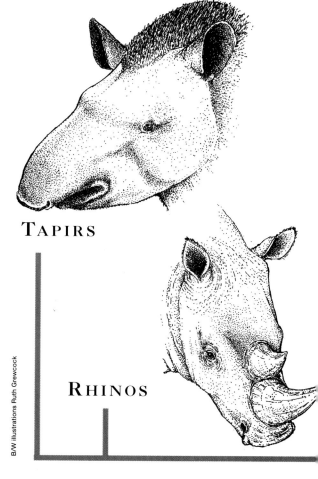

TAPIRS

RHINOS

THE HORSE'S FAMILY TREE

Horses and asses, together with zebras, all belong to the same genus and are related to rhinoceroses and tapirs. Prehistoric species of equid bore stronger physical resemblances to these other animals than is apparent today. Rhinos and tapirs are considerably more heavy-bodied and less well adapted to swift movement; both have three toes on each foot.

ASIATIC WILD ASS

Equus hemionus
(ECK-wus hem-ie-O-nus)

Slightly larger than the African wild ass, this ass's coat color varies according to its location and also, possibly, to the time of year. Upper parts may be a reddish brown, gray, or almost yellow with slightly paler undersides. Generally there is a broad, dark dorsal stripe that may have a paler border, and there may also be a transverse shoulder stripe. This ass has broader feet, a shorter mane and tail, narrower head, and shorter ears than the African wild ass. It is considered to be the swiftest of the wild equids. Four subspecies are generally recognized—the khur, the onager, the kulan, and the dziggetai.

HORSES

ASSES

EQUIDS

AFRICAN WILD ASS

Equus asinus
(ECK-wus Ah-SEEN-us)

In the wild, these animals grow to a height of 49 in (125 cm) at the shoulder with a body length of 78 in (200 cm). They have been bred for centuries for use by humans, and those in domestic situations are generally smaller, varying in height from 30–60 in (80–150 cm). Usually the coat color is gray or a gray-brown, with paler undersides and a dark dorsal stripe running down the back. It has the longest ears proportionately of the wild asses, and its hooves are the narrowest of any of the equids. Sometimes there is also a transverse shoulder stripe and darker bars around the legs. Most authorities recognize three subspecies: Equus asinus atlanticus, E. a. africanus, and E. a. somalicus.

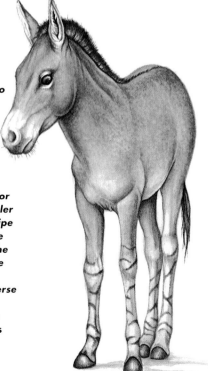

ZEBRAS

ODD-TOED UNGULATES

ANATOMY:
THE PRZHEVALSKI'S HORSE

Przhevalski's horse (right) is medium-sized, standing 47–55 in (120–142 cm) at the withers (shoulder). The smallest horse breed in existence, the Falabella (center), stands 28 in (72 cm) high at the shoulder, while the largest, the Shire (left), averages 67 in (170 cm) at the shoulder.

THE COAT

is a sandy yellow color that merges with its arid background. It may be slightly paler on the underbelly. Usually there is a dark dorsal stripe that extends from the base of the neck along the length of the spine to the tail. Together with the color of the coat, this is a characteristic of a primitive and old type of equid.

VOMERONASAL POUCH

The vomeronasal (voe-mer-o-NAY-zal) pouch lies within the horse's nose and is used to analyze pheromones. In an act known as the flehmen response, a stallion sniffs at a mare's urine, drawing the air into the pouch, to see if she is ready to mate.

THE MANE

runs the length of the neck and is a dark brown or black. Coarse, scrubby hairs stand upright and there is no forelock (hair falling over the face between the ears).

THE FEET

comprise a single toe on each limb, in which the nail has developed into a horny outer wall, known as the hoof. The horse therefore walks on four toes; the added length this gives to each limb increases its ability to move at high speed.

 X RAY

THE SPINE
Long and almost straight, rather than arched as in more primitive equids, the spine allows for speed over a distance rather than a quick, springy start-up movement. There are five sections of vertebral bones. From neck to tail, these are the cervical, dorsal, lumbar, sacral, and caudal vertebrae.

PRZEWALSKI'S HORSE SKELETON

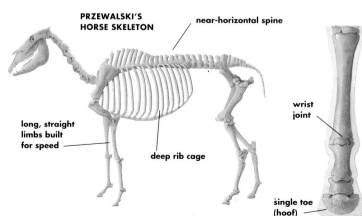

near-horizontal spine

long, straight limbs built for speed

deep rib cage

single toe (hoof)

LEG

In the forelimbs the ulna and radius bones are fused, with the ulna reduced in size. In the hind limbs the tibia and fibula are fused, with the tibia being enlarged. This allows for twisting and turning at high speed with less risk of injury to the ankle and wrist joints. There are strong ligaments in all legs.

wrist joint

Anatomy illustrations Barry Croucher/Wildlife Art Agency

X-ray illustrations Elisabeth Smith

Main illustration Rachel Lockwood/Wildlife Art Agency

FACT FILE:
PRZHEVALSKI'S HORSE

CLASSIFICATION

GENUS: *EQUUS*

SPECIES: *PRZEWALSKII*

SIZE

HEIGHT TO SHOULDER: 47–60 IN (120–142 CM)

HEAD–BODY LENGTH: 85–110 IN (220–280 CM)

TAIL LENGTH: 36–43 IN (92–110 CM)

WEIGHT AT BIRTH: 55–66 LB (25–30 KG)

ADULT WEIGHT: 550–660 LB (250–300 KG)

COLORATION

DUN (SAND-COLORED) COAT WITH PALER UNDERSIDES AND MUZZLE

DARK BROWN OR BLACK MANE, TAIL, AND LEGS

DARK STRIPE DOWN THE CENTER OF THE BACK

FEATURES

LARGE, HEAVY HEAD, USUALLY CONVEX IN PROFILE

COMPARATIVELY LONG, POINTED EARS

LONG, THICKLY HAIRED TAIL, OFTEN SCRUBBY AT THE TOP

LIMBS

The Przhevalski's limbs are usually dark brown or black, but sometimes they have bar markings around them.

THE EARS

are comparatively long and pointed and extremely expressive of a horse's mood. Pricked forward, the animal is alert and attentive. If they are pressed backward, this indicates anger, fear, or aggression.

THE NECK

is thick and comparatively short, with well-developed muscles.

THE MUZZLE

is generally paler than the rest of the coat. The nostrils are large and the upper lip is soft and remarkably mobile.

SKULL

The face is elongated, with the eye socket set high and wide behind the teeth to ensure that there is no pressure on the eyes from the molars. The skull lengthened during the course of evolution to accommodate the large cheek teeth and jawbones. The nasal bones are long and narrow.

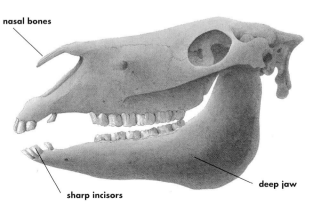

nasal bones

sharp incisors

deep jaw

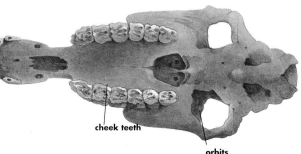

cheek teeth

orbits
(eye sockets)

GLOBAL GRAZERS

TODAY, ALMOST ALL HORSES AND ASSES ARE DOMESTICATED, BUT THEY STILL REMAIN AMONG THE MOST SUCCESSFUL OF GRASSLAND GRAZERS

Man has bred horses and asses for centuries to suit his needs. Today there is a wide variety of breeds in existence, some of which are feral or semiferal. Horses survive well on their own in the North American prairies, in the Camargue Delta of France, areas of the Australian outback, and southwest Africa. Native ponies also roam free in parts of the British Isles, as well as in Iceland.

In a wild or feral state, all equids need shelter, fresh water, and grazing—although many manage to survive in arid, seemingly barren regions. They graze most frequently at dawn and dusk, but may feed at any time of day and night if hunger beckons. They may sleep or doze at any time, too, and will often do so standing up; special locking knee joints keep them from collapsing. They can sleep for as many as seven hours out of the twenty-four. At night, they often lie down to sleep, either on their sides or with their legs gathered underneath them.

FOUR GEARS FOR FLEET FEET

As it grazes, an equid moves at a leisurely walk. If one chases another from a prime piece of grazing, say, or they are alerted, they may trot. Faster still is

Mutual preening is a method of social bonding (right). *It also keeps the skin and coat clean and healthy.*

Exmoor ponies (below) *are native British ponies that can still be found in a semiwild state inhabiting moorland country.*

Robert Maier/Aquila

Robert Maier/Aquila

Feral stallions in the Camargue, France, rear in combat to settle supremacy (below).

Robert Maier/Aquila

the canter, the pace most equids would use in the wild if they were escaping from danger. If need be, they resort to the fastest pace of all—the gallop.

Just how fast an equid can move depends on its type. When Genghis Khan and his "marauding hordes" chased across the plains of Mongolia on the indigenous, small wild horses that existed in his time, they may have reached speeds of 30–37 mph (50–60 km/h). This is almost as fast as a modern racehorse, which may reach 40 mph (65 km/h).

HERDING AND GROOMING

Equids have a natural herding instinct, and in a wild or feral state they normally live in small groups. They all graze separately but keep in constant touch by whinnying softly to one another. If

---

THE ASIATIC WILD ASS, THE SWIFTEST OF THE WILD EQUIDS, CAN REACH SPEEDS OF ABOUT **43 MPH (70 KM/H)**

---

alerted, or if one strays away, the whinnying is louder and more urgent. Members of a herd constantly interact; for example, they often stand head to tail, gently nibbling each other's back and hindquarters with the lips and teeth to remove dead skin and parasites. Alternatively they may just stand quietly in this position, flicking the flies off the other's face with the tail. In addition to performing a service, they can also keep a lookout behind their companion, thereby covering the only blind spot in its field of vision. ∎

HABITATS

Robert Maier/Aquila

Wild horses are most often associated with grasslands. But because they can survive on poorer quality grazing than ruminants, equids have always been able to flourish in more marginal habitats, in areas ranging in climate from tropical to subarctic. They may once have roamed the forests of Europe; the New Forest pony is named after its wooded homeland in southern England.

Horses have become characterized, both in appearance and temperament, according to the natural conditions of their environment. Przhevalski's horse was first discovered in the steppe country of Mongolia, in the Altai Mountains at the edge of the Gobi desert. It actually inhabited the plains and the mountains up to 8,200 ft (2,500 m) in the spring and summer, moving down to about 5,250 ft (1,600 m) as autumn approached. Within these migratory patterns, it seems it would often spend its days in desert areas, then search out places to graze in the late afternoon.

DESERT HORSES

Deserts are hostile environments, but equids have long flourished in arid conditions. The Arabian, one of the oldest of equine breeds, has been a massive

KEY FACTS

- Horses and ponies are distinguished mainly by height. A pony measures no more than 56 in (142 cm) at the withers (the point of the shoulders at the base of the neck); above this, it is a horse. However, horses and ponies possess different characteristics; ponies are generally sharper and more cunning, probably a legacy from their long survival in a feral state.

- Domestic horses and ponies are measured in "hands," one hand being equal to 4 in (10 cm). For its size, the tiny Shetland pony is one of the world's most powerful equines.

- Although standing no higher than 56 in (142 cm), and usually less than this, Przhevalski's horse is never described as a pony.

- The islands of Chincoteague and Assateague, off the coast of Virginia, are home to a herd of small, sturdy ponies. The islands were formed in 1733 when storms tore them from the coast; it is thought the ponies may have swum to the islands from a shipwreck. They live mainly on Assateague but are rounded up and swum across to Chincoteague each year, where some are sold. For the rest of the time they live unaffected by humans, and are said to be some of the last wild stock in the world.

The famous horses of France's Camargue region are rounded up each year, but otherwise they live in a semiwild state in this marshy wilderness.

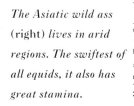

Mark Boulton/Bruce Coleman Ltd.

The Asiatic wild ass (right) lives in arid regions. The swiftest of all equids, it also has great stamina.

DISTRIBUTION

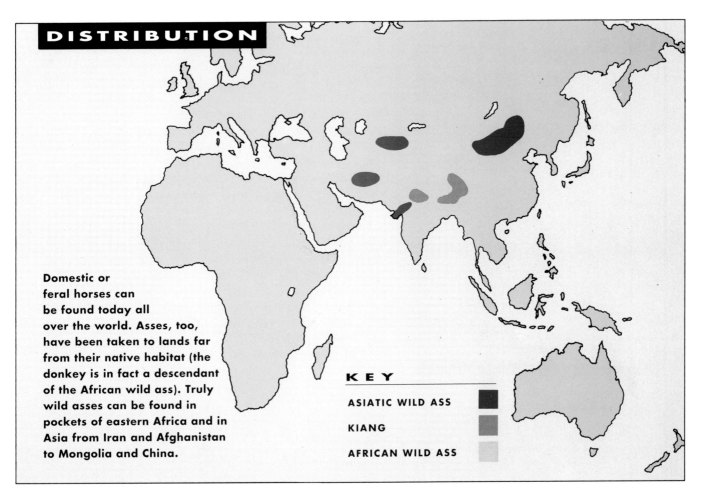

Domestic or feral horses can be found today all over the world. Asses, too, have been taken to lands far from their native habitat (the donkey is in fact a descendant of the African wild ass). Truly wild asses can be found in pockets of eastern Africa and in Asia from Iran and Afghanistan to Mongolia and China.

KEY

ASIATIC WILD ASS

KIANG

AFRICAN WILD ASS

influence on many of today's horse breeds. It has roamed the deserts of the Arabian Peninsula since 2000 B.C. and has always been vital to desert tribes-people. The supreme stamina of Arabian horses is a legacy from their ability to survive such harsh conditions. Two of the most successful of all feral horses—America's mustang and Australia's brumby—live in dusty scrublands, finding shelter where they can. True survivors, these horses tend to have wild natures, making them almost impossible to master.

PONIES OF THE COLD NORTH

The bleak northern tundra has long been a home to horses. The Icelandic horse or pony, a pre-Ice Age equid, has braved the elements in Iceland since it was taken there by Norsemen in the ninth century. The Norwegian Fjord pony is an equid of Norway's lightly forested tundra and was probably an ancestor of the Icelandic horse. Also thought to hail from Scandinavia is the Shetland pony, which has lived in the Shetland Islands, off Scotland, for some 10,000 years. Often its homeland is snowbound for months on end. At such times, the small ponies dig with their hooves to expose grass; they also feed on lichen and bark stripped from trees, and even scavenge on the seashore for seaweed and dead fish.

Many different breeds of horses have made their homes in mountains. The Ariegeois, for example, lives on the eastern Pyrenees of France. This tough little animal is said to be impervious to the iciest of conditions. Similarly, Austria's pony, the Haflinger, survives in the Austrian Tyrol.

Moorland country has always yielded the basic requirements of equids, and most British and Irish native ponies—Dales, Fells, Dartmoor, Exmoor, Connemara, and Welsh Mountain—are inhabitants of this type of environment. Sadly, humans have crossbred them to the degree that few purebred native ponies exist in their habitats today. In most of these areas, however, representatives of the breed still wander apparently wild, although all belong to someone and will be rounded up periodically.

One of the most unusual habitats in which to find equids is the salt marshland of the Camargue region in southern France, where semiwild herds splash through the shallows of the Rhône delta.

The African wild ass probably once occurred in the wild from Morocco to Somalia and from Mesopotamia to Oman. In a semiwild state, it is now found only in remote and arid areas in Africa, in broken, undulating, stony desert country—a reflection on its surefootedness.

FOCUS ON

THE GOBI ALTAI

The inhospitable environment in which Przhevalski's horse was discovered in the 1880s lies at the northwestern edge of the Gobi, where this barren land meets the Altai Mountains of Mongolia. The ancient, rugged Altai ranges extend some 1,200 miles (2,000 km). The highest peaks are more than 13,000 ft (4,000 m) high. There are three main branches of the mountain system—the Gobi, the Mongolian, and the Russian Kazatch Altai. The area known as the Gobi Altai is the westerly extension of the range; these lower mountains gradually level off into the desert. They are known as the Tachin Schara Nuru, or "Mountains of the Yellow Horse," and are crisscrossed by rivers that are often frozen in the winter and dry in the summer. The river valleys support the only farmland in the area, although most of the region's inhabitants are nomadic herders. There are four vegetation zones: mountain subdesert, mountain steppe, mountain forest, and alpine. The first two of these are home to Przhevalski's horse, which moves seasonally between them in search of water and vegetation. Small, shrubby plants grow on the low plains; lower still, scrubby plants grow in the alkaline soils. While forests of conifers, birches, aspens, and larches cover much of the lower Altai regions, there are practically no trees in the Gobi Altai.

TEMPERATURE AND RAINFALL

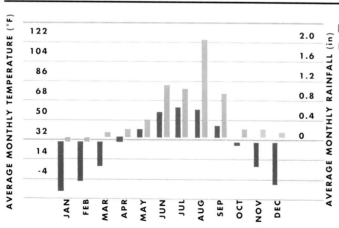

TEMPERATURE
RAINFALL

The Altai Mountains are said to have a continental type of climate, although temperatures can fluctuate to either extreme. The Gobi Altai region has lower rainfall than much of the Altai range—an annual average of 8-10 in (200-250 mm)—and snow may fall in the winter.

The Asiatic wild ass originally lived in deserts, salt flats, and dry steppe country, ranging from the Ukraine and Palestine to Manchuria and western India. Since the turn of this century, it has been reduced to four separate populations—each accounting for one subspecies—in remote areas of China, India, northern Iran, and Turkmenistan.

An inhabitant of high, undulating steppe country is the kiang; the largest of the asses, its nose has a distinctively rounded profile. The kiang is found in Tibet, China, India, and Kashmir at elevations of up to 16,400 ft (5,000 m). ■

NEIGHBORS

Conditions in the Gobi Altai are hostile to wildlife; those species that do survive rely on special adaptations to cope with searing heat in summer and the bitter chill of winter.

JERBOA

This hopping rodent uses its long ears as "radiators" to keep cool. In extreme heat, it hides in its burrow.

SKINK

These short-legged lizards move so effortlessly through the sand that they seem almost to swim.

THE ALTAI MOUNTAINS

The Altai range is as landlocked as almost any part of the Asian landmass. It stretches from Kazakhstan and Russia into western Mongolia, where it tails off into the barren wastes of the Gobi Desert. The western tip of Mongolia is roughly on a latitude with Newfoundland.

RUSSIA

KAZAKH-STAN

ALTAI MOUNTAINS

GOBI

MONGOLIA

CHINA

Bruce Coleman Ltd.

PIKA

The pika is a rabbitlike mountain dweller. Much of its day is spent basking on rocky outcrops.

BUZZARD

In the Gobi Altai, the common buzzard preys on beetles and rodents, and sometimes on small birds.

BACTRIAN CAMEL

This "ship of the desert" still roams wild in the Gobi, using its distinctive two humps as fat stores.

GOITERED GAZELLE

Once widespread, this gazelle has been hunted for food and sport; few now remain in the Gobi region.

EAGLE OWL

A king among owls, the eagle owl is a deadly night hunter, taking prey up to the size of hares.

FOOD AND FEEDING

The principal food for all wild or feral horses is grass, and the need to eat enough of it largely governs their behavior. In areas of poor vegetation, they will wander farther to find grazing and will feed for more hours each day. Where grass is rich and lush, horses generally graze for about 60 percent of the day; as conditions worsen and the grass becomes less nutritious—in autumn and winter, for example—this will increase to 80 percent. Where pastures are really poor, horses will spend up to twenty-two hours a day grazing.

DIGESTING THE ROUGH STUFF
Equids are consummate survivors, even in areas where grazing is sparse, tough, and so low in nutrition that it would seem impossible for such large animals to flourish. In such instances, equids eat whatever they can find: leaves, twigs, fruits, buds, and roots—even lichen and tree bark. The herbage is torn between the strong upper and lower incisors and the sensitive, mobile, rubbery lips help to gather it and push it into the mouth.

By far the biggest group of herbivores are the ruminants: mainly grazing animals that digest their

---

EQUIDS HAVE A VERY LARGE CECUM (PART OF THE COLON), WHERE PROTOZOA AND BACTERIA BREAK DOWN CELLULOSE

---

high-cellulose food by chewing it twice. Most ruminants have four separate stomach chambers, and the food is regurgitated from one of these, the rumen, to be chewed again. Equids have a far simpler, and less efficient, digestive system than that of the ruminants. The fact that they produce much coarser dung bears witness to this. To compensate for this simpler digestion, equids have to eat more than ruminants, and they often graze on vegetation that is too fibrous for ruminants to digest.

Food passes through equids far more rapidly than it does through ruminants (30–45 hours versus 70–100), which also means they can physically eat more each day. Although equids are less efficient at extracting protein from their food, because of their greater capacity and faster rate of digestion, the net result is actually to extract more protein from poorer grazing.

HARDY BROWSERS
Like the horse, the African wild ass is also primarily a grazer, but it will also browse on low vegetation. The ass forages mainly at dawn

INSIGHT

INSIDE A HORSE
A look inside the typical equid reveals that its digestive system is simpler than that of most ruminants. Lacking four stomach chambers to break down tough food, the horse instead has a large gut, or colon, where it processes the grasses it eats. It only partly digests the food, but by excreting the waste soon afterward, it manages to pass a great deal of food through its body each day.

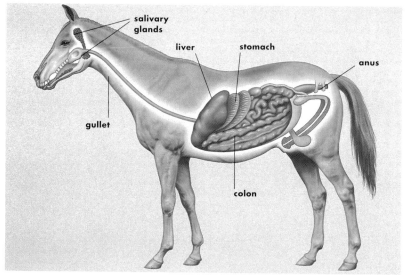

salivary glands
liver
stomach
anus
gullet
colon

Steve Kingston

A FAMILY HERD
of African wild asses graze on scrub in Somalia.

Przhevalski's horse can go without water for longer periods than domestic breeds. In the kiang's native habitat, vegetation is at its most abundant in August and September. This ass takes advantage of the bounty and feeds long hours at this time of year, often gaining 90–100 lb (40–45 kg) within a few weeks.

GRAZERS WITH BIFOCALS

Lowering its long neck and head to feed, a grazing horse might seem to the casual observer to be oblivious to the world around it—and oblivious to predators. But this is not the case. As the horse grazes, its long ears are constantly flicking back and forth, listening intently for warning sounds, and it also possesses a sight advantage. The upper half of the retina in the eye is farther from the

---

STRONG INCISORS HELP EQUIDS TO CROP TOUGH, TALL GRASSES, TWIGS, AND ROOTS, AS WELL AS THE SOFT, SHORT GRASS EATEN BY RUMINANTS

---

lens than the lower half; this has a similar effect to a pair of bifocal glasses. As a result, while its head is lowered, the animal can not only see the grass it is eating, but, at the same time, it can focus clearly on objects some distance away with the top half of the eye. So even while grazing in comfort, the horse can keep a wary lookout for trouble on the horizon. ∎

A New Forest pony (below) *grazes in a field of heather in Hampshire, England.*

SHETLAND

ponies rake at the snow to find grass (above).

and during the late afternoon, tending to rest quietly in the midday heat. Studies reveal that some 60 percent of its food intake is from grazing on grasses, sedges, and other herbage, while 40 percent comes from browsing on low-level shrubs.

The Asiatic wild ass feeds mainly on grasses and low succulent plants, but it has been known to survive well on straw, which contains very little nutritive value. Although the ass can survive for longer than most horses without drinking, a high thirst will compel it to search widely for water, particularly in the summer. Among horses,

Main illustrations Kim Thompson

Robert Maier/Aquila

SOCIAL STRUCTURE

Equids are gregarious animals, although horses and asses tend to adopt slightly differing social structures. Horses in the wild live in small herds comprising a few mares with their offspring of up to two or three years, dominated by a stallion. Often the mares stay in this herd all their lives, even if the stallion is ousted by a younger one. The herd wanders over a home range, the size of which varies according to the quality of the grazing. Their need for fresh water limits them to sites within 12–18 miles (20–30 km) of a water source. The home range may overlap with other herds and is not defended as such; fights occur between stallions usually only when one is challenging for leadership of a group.

Young stallions form bachelor herds; these are unstable, for its members soon try to steal mares from other herds to form their own harems. There may also be groups of young horses of about three years old that have left their parental herd but have yet to enter more permanent associations.

HERD HABITS

Family herds are close-knit, resting, feeding, and roaming together and grooming one another. They tend to communicate through vocalizations. Often, when the herd is stationary, individuals will take a dust bath, a typically equine practice in which the animal gets down on its side and rolls on the dusty ground. It then rubs its head and body against trees or rocks to relieve minor irritations. Members of a herd may even line up at a particularly good dust-bathing spot.

If the dominant stallion plans to move the herd on, or if he suspects trouble from enemies, he rounds up his herd, sometimes aided by a few young males, and sends them on. The herd is then generally led by the most dominant mare, with the stallion bringing up the rear.

RIVALRY

Life in the herd is usually peaceful, although there is a pecking order—for both mares and stallions. Age, size, and length of time in the group helps to establish dominance, but so, too, does aggression. Confrontations range from threatening facial expressions to actual fights. A high position in the herd is desirable; those at the top get the best choice of grazing and first position at a water hole, and they are the ones most likely to breed. When a young stallion challenges for supremacy of a herd, the fighting is violent. Unlike

Main illustrations John Cox/Wildlife Art Agency

the mares, stallions are armed with large, spade-shaped canines, which rarely draw blood but can deliver a nasty nip. Although success in a fight depends as much on agility as strength, it is quite unusual for a dominant stallion to lose control of a herd. Instead, most young stallions establish their own harems by enticing young mares from other established or unstable

FIGHTING

stallions kick and bite, watched from a safe distance by the victor's prize—a herd of mares.

*in*SIGHT

VOCALIZATIONS

Among the equids, horses are particularly vocal. As two herd members meet, they may whicker softly before touching noses. A soft blowing sound uttered by a grazing horse suggests contentment. Contact over some distance is maintained with a loud whinny, whereas an alert to danger is usually given by a loud snort. Fighting is accompanied by squeals of varying frenzy.

Robert Maier/Aquila

herds. The mares within an established herd also guard their positions jealously and react aggressively to any intruders—male or female.

ASS ASSOCIATIONS

African and Asiatic wild ass herds tend to be looser than those of horses. Adult males establish a territory, in which they tolerate the presence of subordinate males, except during the breeding season. Females and young bachelor males form large, unstable groups, which may form in the morning and disband by the evening. They graze and rest together, and will even flee en masse from any threat or danger, but there is little of the mutual grooming or greeting that there is among horses.

A dominant male's territory may be up to nine square miles (23 square kilometers). Wandering herds often have to pass through this area to get to good grazing and water, which gives the dominant male access to those females for breeding. ■

KEY FACTS

● When two Przhevalski's stallions greet each other, one generally displays submission by lowering its head and making gentle chewing motions with an open mouth.

● Equids are naturally curious but also fearful. Any unusual movement will instantly attract a group of horses, which will all lift their heads and strain their ears forward for sounds. Often this is accompanied by defecation and urination—a precaution taken in case flight is required.

● All equids can swim, but above all of them the kiang seems to take positive pleasure from this activity and will often swim across rivers in its path.

● Asses make very different sounds from horses; they bray, whereas horses whinny.

LIFE CYCLE

Equids can breed all year round, but in the wild they will all give birth when grazing conditions are at their best. In the feral mustangs of America, for example, births tend to peak from April to June. Przhevalski's horses normally produce their foals at this time of year, too. The African wild ass usually gives birth during the wet season in its native habitat, while the Asiatic wild ass usually produces its foals from late April to October. For the kiang, mating takes place in mid-September, with birth occurring the following July or August. Courtship and mating rituals among these animals depend slightly on their herd arrangement.

The dominant stallion in a herd has access to the mares in his group, although he may have to fend off many rivals. As the mares come into estrus, the stallion repeatedly checks their urine (see page 1022). If he judges a mare ready, mating will follow. Gestation varies: In Przhevalski's horse, it is about 335 days; domestic horses gestate for 315–387 days according to the breed, and asses for 330-360 days.

AS MARES

come into estrus, fights break out between stallions for mating rights; these can be very violent.

DOMINANT MALE ASSES ARE BESET BY RIVALS, WHO COMPETE FOR THE RIGHT TO MATE WITH THE RECEPTIVE FEMALES

Most equid mares leave the herd to give birth (kiang mares sometimes go off in small groups at this time), seeking a sheltered spot among rocks, trees, or tall grasses. The mare generally lies down to give birth, then stays with the foal, letting it take its first drink of her rich milk.

YOUNG MARES

generally leave the herd when they become sexually mature, often lured or stolen away by young stallions. Young stallions also leave when sexually mature, forming bachelor groups until they establish harems of their own.

THE NEWBORN FOAL

In all species, the foal can stand within minutes of birth; it can walk and run soon afterward; its ears and eyes are open; it can urinate and defecate by itself; and it is able to regulate its own body temperature. This is typical of herd animals whose main form of defense is to run from predators. However, the foal is born toothless. Its incisors start to appear at about ten days old, and it has a full set of milk teeth at about six months old. Like humans, it gradually loses these, growing all its adult teeth by the time it is five or six years old.

This Arabian foal is already displaying the elegant proportions of its breed as it canters alongside its mother.

Fritz Prenzel/Tony Stone Worldwide

BIRTHS

occur in a sheltered spot, usually a little way away from the remainder of the grazing herd. The foal is born with all its senses operating and can stand and follow its mother within a short time of birth.

THE MARE

and foal rejoin the herd shortly after birth. Foals quickly interact with other youngsters in the group, gamboling while mares graze peacefully nearby.

Illustration Robin Budden/Wildlife Art Agency

WHEN MOVING,

a foal stays by its mother's side. If there is danger around, the other herd members will close around the youngsters, giving them extra protection.

GROWTH OF A FOAL

Newborn foals have disproportionately long legs to help them run with the herd to escape danger. At one year old, they still appear leggy and slender; the muscling process takes at least another two years.

The long leg bones are not fully formed and strengthened until the animal is about two years old. Until this time, a horse cannot do long, hard work; if forced to do so, there is a high risk of damage or even deformation to the legs.

FROM BIRTH TO DEATH

PRZHEVALSKI'S HORSE
GESTATION: AVERAGE 335 DAYS
NUMBER OF YOUNG: 1
BREEDING: MATING AND BIRTHS OCCUR FROM APRIL TO JUNE

SEXUAL MATURITY: MALES 4–5 YEARS, FEMALES 3–4 YEARS
LONGEVITY: MAXIMUM RECORDED 34 YEARS

AFRICAN WILD ASS
GESTATION: USUALLY 1 YEAR
NUMBER OF YOUNG: 1
BREEDING: THROUGHOUT YEAR, BUT BIRTH GENERALLY COINCIDES WITH RAINY SEASON

SEXUAL MATURITY: MALES 2–3 YEARS, FEMALES 1–2 YEARS
LONGEVITY: MAXIMUM RECORDED IN DOMESTICATED STATE 47 YEARS

ASIATIC WILD ASS
GESTATION: AVERAGE 330 DAYS
NUMBER OF YOUNG: 1
BREEDING: MATING OCCURS FROM MARCH TO SEPTEMBER

SEXUAL MATURITY: MALES 2–3 YEARS, FEMALES 1–2 YEARS
LONGEVITY: MAXIMUM RECORDED IN DOMESTICATED STATE 35 YEARS

Mares and their newborn foals rejoin the herd as soon as possible to benefit from the protection of numbers. Equine mares are protective, calling their young to them when alarmed and aggressively repelling intruders. Foals run alongside their mothers when the herd is on the move, but at other times they often stray a little way away, prancing and leaping with the other youngsters of the herd.

TO PROTECT HER FOAL, A MARE WILL CHARGE AT UNWELCOME VISITORS, BITING AND KICKING THEM TO DRIVE THEM AWAY

Foals start to graze at about six weeks old. Most continue to suckle for up to a year, although in domestic situations many will be weaned before this. Both sexes usually leave the herd upon reaching sexual maturity; females are usually lured away to a harem, while young males bond together until they are mature enough to form herds of their own.

BREEDING CAPABILITIES

Sexual maturity is reached at different ages according to species. African and Asiatic wild mares seem able to breed in their second year, males a year later. The kiang probably breeds a little later. Przewalski's mares become mature at three to four years old, and males a year later. Mares of domestic breeds can produce young when they are two, and stallions are sexually mature at one, but breeding is generally delayed for a while. In theory all species could produce young each year, since they come into estrus a few days after they give birth; in practice most births occur every other year. All species usually give birth to a single young; when twins are conceived, they often do not develop to term. ∎

THE WORLD'S CARRIERS

AS WITH SO MANY WILD ANIMALS, IT IS MAN WHO HAS BEEN RESPONSIBLE FOR THE DEMISE OF HORSES AND ASSES IN THEIR NATURAL ENVIRONMENT. NOW ONLY HE CAN SAVE THEM

Of all the animals that have ever lived in the world, it must surely be horses and asses that have done the most to shape man's future as he has tamed them to work for him. Apart from being beasts of burden and transport to carry or pull people and their belongings from place to place, they have been used by humans to help them cultivate the land since time immemorial. Horses have also long been one of the key components in many areas of sport,s by which many people earn a living and on which countless others rely to occupy and amuse themselves in their leisure time.

TWIST OF FATE

Yet in spite of this, the fate of horses and asses today must constitute one of the greatest ironies in the natural world. It is conceivable that there are more horses alive in modern times than there have been at any time throughout their history, and yet whether any can be termed truly wild is doubtful. Asses do still survive in the wild, probably because they have not shown the same diversification in breeding programs as has been found in the many guises of the horse.

The discovery of Przhevalski's horse by Colonel Przhevalski toward the end of the 19th century in the Altai Gobi region of the Mongolian steppes brought some negative attention but ultimately may have saved the species from extinction. The hardy little animal was, of course, well known to local tribespeople, who had used it for generations. After its discovery, however, it naturally attracted worldwide interest, as the discovery of any new wild animal would. It was sought by zoos and wild animal collectors the world over, and the local tribespeople were only too happy to supply the need that brought them financial gain. In addition, as agriculture spread increasingly across the steppe land, so the herds of wild horses came to be regarded as ever more of a nuisance. Not only did they compete with domestic stock for grazing, but they would also break into enclosures to gain access to the domesticated mares, often luring them away to a life of freedom on the steppes beyond.

Fortunately, the fact that Przhevalski's horse was collected and sent to zoos has saved the breed. In particular, thirteen horses were taken in the middle of this century and kept in captivity; from these have descended the 1,000 or so purebred Przhevalski's horses living today, and there are also campaigns to put some of these animals back into the wild.

A brumby foal in Fraser Island, Queensland (right). *Brumbies are feral descendants of workhorses brought to Australia during the gold rush.*

ANT/NHPA

Rod Williams/Bruce Coleman Ltd.

A Przhevalski's horse with foal (above). *Life in zoos has saved this horse from complete extinction, and it is now being reintroduced into the wild.*

This map shows the range of Przhevalski's horse in the mid-19th century and where it was last sighted.

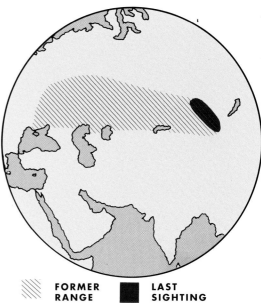

⟋⟋ **FORMER RANGE**   ■ **LAST SIGHTING**

It is thought that on its discovery, Przhevalski's horse had already been pushed to the fringe desert zones of the steppe lands where it was found. Then, only a decade or two later, it was known to be rare in its already reduced native environment. By the 1950s, the encroaching agriculture pushed it farther back into a small part of southwestern Mongolia and nearby China. The last confirmed sighting in the wild came in 1968 in southwestern Mongolia.

Of the asses, it seems that the kiang is probably surviving in the greatest numbers in the wild. Recent estimates put its numbers at 250,000 still roaming parts of eastern central Asia, including Tibet, China, parts of the former USSR, and Mongolia. The reason for its apparent success is probably its inhospitable and remote habitat—high altitudes and barren ground where little grows—which discourages much in the way of penetration by people. However, the kiang may have suffered since the Chinese occupation of Tibet, which has brought with it a certain amount of agricultural and industrial development. This means that not only is there now increased competition for the grazing, but there is also less grazing land available to fight over.

It seems that the Asiatic wild ass, now found in four separate locations, once occupied a huge part

SPECIES

ENDANGERED

of the Eurasian arid zone, roaming from Palestine to the Gobi in great numbers. It, too, of course, has been domesticated for centuries by locals and other people, and has also come into conflict with man, who has developed much of its homeland. Besides being captured and domesticated, it has been widely hunted across its range for food and skins, as well as, surprisingly, for sport. It had probably been pushed out of much of its range in the European part of the former USSR as early as the 17th or 18th century, and it followed suit in Kazakhstan and central Asia soon after. By the beginning of the 20th century, truly wild Asiatic wild asses were extinct in Kazakhstan.

Nowadays most Asiatic wild asses survive in protected reserves, where estimates put their existing numbers at around 2,000. Other sources, however, claim that there are still 3,860 square miles (100,000 square kilometers) of natural habitat in Mongolia, where the Asiatic wild ass may be found, and they put the numbers of animals in existence there at 5,000–6,000.

The African wild ass, it seems, has fared even less fortunately, and many experts consider it to be on the verge of extinction in its natural habitat in northeastern Africa. At best, it is thought that no

---

THE AFRICAN WILD ASS HAS FALLEN VICTIM TO DISEASES SPREAD BY DOMESTIC LIVESTOCK. IT HAS ALSO BEEN WIDELY CROSSBRED WITH THE DOMESTIC DONKEY

---

more than 1,000 survive and probably considerably fewer. The same factors have brought it to this state as have affected the other wild equids—namely, hunting and habitat reduction as well as widespread domestication.

PROUD, FREE SPIRITS

Best known among the feral horses in the world today are probably America's mustang (see America's Wild Horses, right), Australia's brumby, and southern France's Camarguais. More than the native ponies of Britain, which may be seen in small numbers wandering in their respective areas from time to time, these three breeds symbolize the proud, free spirit of the horse. Nevertheless, the first two in particular, having been introduced to their newfound homelands by humans, have since suffered greatly at their hands.

As in the United States, throughout the history of man, horses were unknown in the Australian continent until explorers from Spain and Holland first introduced them in the 16th century. As more settlers and British convicts arrived in greater

ANT/NHPA

AMERICA'S WILD HORSES

The open prairies of America's "wild" west have long been home to a much admired horse—one that has come to be known as the mustang. Like the brumby, it lacks unifying characteristics of appearance, for it has descended in a wild and free state from horses that were brought to the United States at the beginning of the 16th century by the Spanish Conquistadores.

HORSE THIEVES

It was the North American indians who were mainly responsible for the mustang's prolific and rapid spread over the lands west of the Mississippi. Although they had never seen horses before, the Indians quickly became superb horsemen.

Vast numbers of the horses acquired by the Indians escaped to a life of freedom in the prairies. Clearly the environment suited these

CONSERVATION MEASURES

Initially the mustang's future rested with private protection associations, such as the Spanish Mustang Registry, Wyoming. In Nevada, the International Society for the Protection of Mustangs and Burros campaigned for more ranges for wild horses on public lands. As a result:

● The U.S. Wild Free-roaming Horse and Burro Act of 1971 made it a federal offense to harass or

feral horses, for they bred rapidly. As the white man put a stop to the traditions of the American Indians, so the horses multiplied even faster, no longer used by the Indians as mounts. Some animals, of course, became the typical horse of the cowboy, but as this way of life also dwindled, or became increasingly reliant on mechanization, mustangs proliferated in even greater numbers.

By the beginning of the 20th century, there were estimated to be about one million horses roaming the grasslands of western America. To the ranchers they were nothing but a nuisance, and, as in Australia, the ranchers began to take things into their own hands. Many more mustangs met their end toward the end of World War I, when they were killed to provide food for European populations.

By 1970, the herds were devastated, and remarkably few of these robust, elegant horses remained. Federal and state laws, classifying them as domestic animals gone wild, would not give them the protection they had been prepared to give to "wildlife." It was estimated that if they had not been given immediate legal status and protection, mustangs would have been virtually eliminated by the end of the 1970s.

TODAY, THE MUSTANG—A SYMBOL OF THE WILD WEST—CAN ROAM IN PROTECTED RESERVES, SUCH AS THIS ONE IN WYOMING.

Inset Tony Stone Worldwide

kill a wild horse. It also protected the wild asses of the same prairies—again descendants from Spanish stock—which were valued as a historic symbol.

● Today, several free-ranging herds of asses are maintained in protected reserves. Studies of these and free-living mustang herds provide important information on how these animals live in the wild.

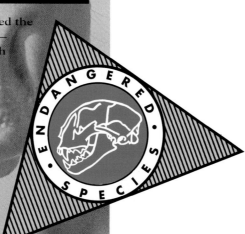

HORSES IN DANGER

THE CHART BELOW SHOWS HOW THE INTERNATIONAL UNION FOR THE CONSERVATION OF NATURE (IUCN), OR THE WORLD CONSERVATION UNION, CLASSIFIES THE STATUS OF PRZHEVALSKI'S HORSE (THE ONLY LIVING HORSE TO BE CONSIDERED WILD) AND ASSES IN THE WILD.

PRZHEVALSKI'S HORSE	EXTINCT IN NATURE, SAVED IN CAPTIVITY
ASIATIC WILD ASS	VULNERABLE

IN ADDITION, TWO SUBSPECIES OF THE ASIATIC WILD ASS, *EQUUS HEMIONUS HEMIPPUS* AND *E. H. KHUR*—THE SYRIAN AND INDIAN WILD ASSES—ARE CONSIDERED EXTINCT IN SYRIA AND ENDANGERED IN PAKISTAN AND INDIA RESPECTIVELY.

Steven C. Kaufman/Bruce Coleman Ltd.

numbers, and there came a need to cultivate the land, so the need for horses became more acute, leading to further importations from Europe.

BACK TO THE BUSH

In the centuries that followed, people flocked to the great Australian outback to look for gold. This influx reached its zenith in the mid-19th century and prospectors took to the bush in the hundreds, using horses and asses. Inevitably, some animals escaped into the surrounding countryside, where they quickly reverted to a wild state.

Conditions in the Australian outback were—and still are—very poor grazing, dry land, and often a scarcity of water. In such circumstances, it is the toughest, most wily animals that survive and go on to breed. The resulting stock, which came to be called brumbies, were a race of hardy scrub horses with high intelligence—or survival instincts—but of nondescript appearance and little in the way of unifying conformation or features. Their numbers were to swell following World War I when mechanization superseded the horses that had been used in agricultural development, and many of these were also turned out into the bush.

By the 1960s, Australia's feral horses were considered a nuisance by farmers and large property owners; they trampled the pastures and ate the grazing earmarked for domestic stock, made short work of fences in their way, churned up the water holes, and frequently lured domestic mares away

MODERN HORSE BREEDS

There are some 200 breeds and types of horses in the world today. Some, such as the Camarguais, have evolved naturally; others have been bred selectively.

Horses are bred for speed, stamina, strength, agility, and beauty. Besides the actual breeds recognized—horses that have a breed society, a stud book, and typical breed characteristics—there are also a number of other types. These are often horses of mixed parentage, bred for a specific equestrian activity, such as hunting, eventing, or showing. Also not a recognized breed are horses and ponies known as palominos, indicating a color rather than a type. The typical palomino is a pale sandy color with a silvery white mane and tail.

Among the most famous of all breeds is the Thoroughbred, first produced in England but now bred in most countries of the world. Although used widely in equestrian sports, it is probably best known on the racetrack, having been bred for speed and athleticism. It came into existence in the 18th century following the import into England of its three foundation sires—the Darley and Godolphin Arabians and the Byerley Turk. Thoroughbred breeding is now a major industry, with horses changing hands for huge sums of money.

Fritz Peenze/Tony Stone Worldwide

A palomino colt (above), whose distinctive color can range from a light to dark golden hue.

The Camarguais (below) survive on the reedy pastures of the salt marsh.

Robert Maier/Aquila

into the bush. War was waged on them and a new living sprang up for the outback "cowboys," who became known as brumby-runners. They would round up the wild horses, trapping them in corrals. The best would be sold as saddle horses (although the brumby is notoriously difficult to train) while the others would be shot and usually sold for pet food. By the 1970s, the brumby was largely extinct, and few remain free in the Australian outback today.

RUNNING WILD

The white horses of the Ile de la Camargue region in southern France are still described today as being half wild. They live in the swampy marshes of the Rhône delta area in much the same way they have done for centuries. No one knows for sure just how long the Camarguais horses have lived here, but they undoubtedly represent a breed of great antiquity and bear more than a passing resemblance to the horses depicted in the cave paintings in Lascaux, France, which are known to be some 17,000 years old.

The story of the Camarguais is an infinitely happier one than that of the mustang or brumby. These magnificent horses are such an integral part of this area, and so important to its life and local tradition, that, although they are left to live relatively free, they are also well protected. If there is known to be conflict between stallions fighting over harems, for example, the protagonists will be separated and placed in well-distanced areas with a harem of twenty or so mares each. They are then left to breed in free-ranging herds, surviving with little interference from man on the poor, reedy pastures of the salt marsh. ■

INTO THE FUTURE

Since the middle of this century, Przhevalski's horse has survived mainly in zoos. It has been found to breed well in captivity—considerably better than many wild animals. A painstaking program of using purebred stock, with mares being carefully selected through the help of computer programs for good genetic health, has resulted in the breed being kept pure. As a result, there are now over 1,000 Przhevalski's horses in zoos around the world.

SURVIVAL OF THE TOUGHEST

However, it is this very selection, which has been so successful in captivity, that could spell disaster in the wild. Releasing animals back into the wild, where they fend totally for themselves,

PREDICTION

DESTINATION ASIA

Attempts are already under way to reintroduce the Przhevalski horse to the wild in Mongolia and Siberia. The captive population has provided a second chance for the survival of the species.

is never easy. Where those that survive in the wild do so because of their toughness and aggressive nature, the reverse is true in zoos. In the restricted confines and artificially controlled atmosphere of a zoo, selection pressures are different. Current breeding plans emphasize retention of genetic diversity and avoid any overt attempts at selection, but it is an inescapable fact that management by humans in no way equals natural selection in the wild.

In an initial experiment, males have been released to test the suitability of the environment. If they prove adaptable and survive easily, mares will be released to form their own breeding groups and will be left entirely alone to live and select males by themselves.

Although return to the wild is necessarily full of danger, it does mean that Przhevalski's horse has some hope of survival in its native environment, and will not be preserved simply as a curiosity in a zoo. ■

BORN TO BE WILD

Within the last few years, fearing that Przhevalski's horse may be extinct in the wild, there have been plans to reintroduce it into the wild.

Experiments to this end began at an equine research station in Arles, France. Initial studies were made of Camargue horses in their natural habitat; groups were left entirely alone for five years, during which time it was discovered that they reverted to their wild social groupings and habits.

It was then decided to release some Przhevalski's horses into a reserved habitat of wild, rugged terrain in Cevennes, France, in the southern part of the Massif Central. The area was chosen because it has many of the rugged characteristics of, and a similar altitude to, the area in Mongolia where Przhevalski's horse was first found.

Another experiment, conducted some 1,000 miles (1,600 km) to the east in Askania Nova, part of the Ukraine, boasts the largest herd of Przhevalski's horses found anywhere—some 10 percent of the world's total. The area where this herd is living, comprising about 3,700 acres (1,500 hectares), is said to be almost the only bit of true grassland steppe left in Europe, the rest having been developed for agriculture.

Here there are three breeding herds and one bachelor herd. The breeding herds are considerably larger than they would be in a truly wild situation. Instead of having three or four mares, these stallions have up to ten. The bachelor herd of about a dozen young males lives in close proximity to the breeding herds. Although they are managed—the sizes of the herds are controlled, for example—these horses are left to live as wild and naturally as possible.

As these horses breed and produce more Przhevalski's horses, and space runs out for them in Askania Nova, there are plans to take them and release them in other areas, specifically in central Mongolia and the Siberian steppes—the true homes of this animal.

Illustration Steve Kingston

HYENAS

Gunter Ziesler/Bruce Coleman Ltd.

Hyenas are members of the order Carnivora, which includes the cats, dogs, bears, raccoons, weasels, and civets. Each group is a family of closely related species. The hyena family is the smallest, with four species in three genera.

ORDER

Carnivora
(carnivores)

FAMILY

Hyaenidae
(hyenas)

SPECIES

Crocuta crocuta
(spotted hyena)

Hyaena brunnea
(brown hyena)

Hyaena hyaena
(striped hyena)

Proteles cristatus
(aardwolf)

BONE CRACKERS

WITH THEIR MASSIVE TEETH, POWERFUL JAWS, AND ACID-BATH DIGESTIVE SYSTEMS, HYENAS ARE SUPERBLY EQUIPPED TO MAKE A LIVING OUT OF THE DEBRIS THAT OTHER PREDATORS DISCARD AS INEDIBLE

Out in the dark, the hyenas are on the prowl. Moonlight silvers their bristling manes, outlining their long, mobile necks and sloping backs as they lope across the savanna. One pauses, turns its heavy muzzle into the wind to sniff the air, then lowers its head to call: an eerie, rising whoop. It can smell blood. The others sniff too—somewhere out there a cheetah has killed a gazelle. The clan moves off, following the scent trail as it grows thicker. They will soon chase off the cheetah, and before long the gazelle will be reduced to a smear of blood, a few tufts of hair, and a pair of horns.

Hyenas are the butchers of the plains. Evolution has equipped them with viselike jaws studded with immense teeth capable of crushing the bones of a buffalo. Their digestive systems are among the most efficient of all carnivores, able to process skin, bone, and even teeth, allowing them to thrive on the animal debris that other predators abandon.

This capacity for eating the uneatable makes them superb scavengers, and as a result they have acquired a macabre reputation for devouring the rotting remains of the dead. In Africa and India they are accused of entering graveyards to feast on corpses. According to African mythology, witches ride their backs.

Like many popular images of wild animals, such myths are somewhat distorted. Of the four species in the hyena family, only two—the brown hyena and the striped hyena—are full-time scavengers. The spotted hyena is an accomplished predator that

HYENAS HAVE A HIGHLY ACUTE SENSE OF SMELL, FOR THE DETECTION OF FOOD, RIVALS, AND POTENTIAL MATES

often hunts in packs like the wolf, while the aardwolf lives almost exclusively upon termites, which it licks up with its long, sticky tongue.

The four species are classified together in the family Hyaenidae (hie-EEN-id-ie) because they share anatomical features that indicate a common ancestry: certain characteristics of the inner ear bones and, more obviously, special pouches under their tails that secrete a pungent paste used for scent marking. And while hyenas are superficially doglike, comparative anatomy suggests that their closest relatives are the civets, genets, and mongooses of the family Viverridae (viv-AIR-rid-ie).

Jonathan Scott/Planet Earth Pictures

The spotted hyena is often found in the vicinity of a source of fresh water.

DIGESTION

Dieter and Mary Plage/Survival Anglia

The digestive powers of a spotted hyena are awe inspiring. The bones of a victim are crushed and bolted down along with the skin, flesh, and entrails, leaving only the horns and tail hairs. The carcass may have been lying around for days in the hot sun, stinking and shunned by other animals, but the hyena's stomach can cope with anything. Even teeth are broken down for the nutrients they contain.

Only the hair is rejected. Along with fragments of bone and hoof, it is regurgitated as pellets. Hyenas are the only carnivores to do this, and it may be the reason why they do not regurgitate food for their cubs. Instead, the mother spotted hyena feeds the young on milk for 9 to 16 months—a long lactation that may be made possible by all the calcium-rich bones in her diet.

The bones and teeth of the earliest identifiable hyenas, dating from some 20 million years ago, suggest that they were tree-dwelling animals resembling the modern banded civet, with an omnivorous diet of small vertebrates, insects, carrion, and fruit.

Later species such as *Ictitherium* (ick-ti-THEER-ee-um), dating from 15 million years ago, were more like dogs or foxes, with a relatively slender, graceful build and well-proportioned limbs. Most of these lightweight hyenas have disappeared—possibly through competition with the true dogs that invaded

The brown hyena is a true scavenger of the arid habitats in which it is found.

D. & R. Sullivan/Bruce Coleman Ltd.

THE HYENA'S FAMILY TREE

the Old World from North America some five to seven million years ago—but the type persists in the foxlike aardwolf, which survived because it became a specialist at hunting termites.

Meanwhile another strain of hyenas had arisen. There was an opening for creatures that could process the corpses left behind by the saber-toothed cats, crunching through bones and processing the nutrients they contained. The hyenas filled the niche with species like *Pachycrocuta* (pak-ee-crock-YOO-ta), a super-scavenger that weighed in at 440 lb (200 kg)—more than twice the weight of the modern spotted hyena.

Surviving skulls of *Pachycrocuta* vividly illustrate the crucial adaptations that made hyenas what they are today. The jaw is relatively short and heavily muscled to give an immensely powerful bite, and while the front incisor and canine teeth are normal enough, the premolar teeth have become great cones of ivory capable of splintering the leg bones of an elephant. At the back of the jaw, behind the bone crackers, lie a set of scissor-like carnassials for shearing through meat.

Pachycrocuta disappeared during the ice ages, but its role was inherited by the smaller spotted hyena. It has the same massive skull, short jaw, and immense bone-cracking teeth, as well as the sharp, meat-shearing carnassials at the back of the mouth. If necessary it will hunt as well as scavenge, and in many parts of Africa it is the most important predator on the plains.

The striped and brown hyenas are more lightly built and less heavily armed. They have the same arrangement of cheek teeth, but they use them all for bone cracking. The carnassials at the back have become stronger and blunter, and are no longer so effective as meat slicers. Accordingly they specialize in processing the bones of carrion, although these animals will also take small live animals.

All three species of "true" hyenas have powerful forequarters, long front legs, and long, strong necks for lifting carrion clear off the ground and carrying it away. Their hind legs are comparatively short and slight, giving them a sloping profile and a curiously underdeveloped appearance at the rear end.

Hyenas' senses are acute. Their smell-detecting nasal membranes are 50 times the size of ours, and they move through a world of complex fragrances. They can see in the dark like cats, and their hearing is excellent. Even as they sleep, hyenas are monitoring the air for the scent and sound of sudden death in the night.

The four species of hyenas can be divided into three basic types: the aardwolf (genus Proteles), *the spotted hyena (genus* Crocuta), *and the brown and striped hyenas (genus* Hyaena). *The aardwolf is a direct but highly adapted descendant of the slender, doglike hyenas of the distant past. The spotted hyena represents the heavyweight hunter-scavenger type that superseded them, while the brown and striped hyenas are closely related, smaller species with more omnivorous tastes.*

AARDWOLF
Proteles cristatus
(*pro-TEE-lees cris-TA-tus*)

Highly adapted for feeding on termites, the aardwolf is quite unlike any other living hyenid. It is small and doglike in build, with reduced teeth and big ears for detecting the sound of foraging termites.

Ⓐ NCESTORS

The ultimate ancestor of all hyenas probably lived in trees, but the earliest recognizable hyenid is *Ictitherium*, a jackal-like animal whose fossils have been found in Greece in rocks laid down some 15 million years ago. Lightly built, with teeth resembling those of a dog, *Ictitherium* and similar species probably lived by a mixture of scavenging and small-game hunting much like today's wild dogs. Ultimately outclassed by the true dogs, most of these doglike hyenas became extinct some five million years ago. In terms of bone cracking, scavenging, and termite eating, modern hyenas are not in direct competition with the lifestyle of dogs and wolves.

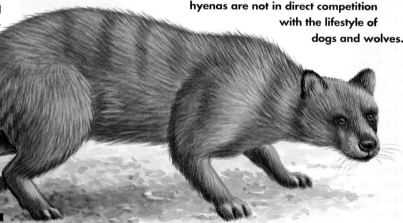

All illustrations Mike Donnelly/Wildlife Art Agency

STRIPED HYENA
Hyaena hyaena
(hie-EE-na hie-EE-na)

The only hyena found in Asia as well as Africa, this is an opportunist scavenger that was once frequently seen raiding garbage dumps on the outskirts of Indian cities. Shy and scarce throughout its broad range, relatively little is known of its habits.

SPOTTED HYENA
Crocuta crocuta
(crock-YOO-ta crock-YOO-ta)

The biggest, strongest, and most aggressive of all the hyenas, this species lives in highly social clans and feeds mainly on large grazing animals on the African savannas. In many areas it hunts in packs; it is the most successful of all African predators.

BROWN HYENA
Hyaena brunnea
(hie-EE-na brun-AE-a)
This hyena lives in the deserts of southwest Africa. It also occurs on the Atlantic coast of Namibia, where it is called the beachwolf.

EARLY HYENIDS
(e.g. Ictitherium)

A N A T O M Y :
THE HYENAS

AARDWOLF COAT

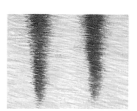

The striped coat may have developed in mimicry of the bigger striped hyena, but it more probably represents a form of ancestral hyenid coat pattern.

MANE

Under threat, the thick mane of coarse hair can be bristled up to make the striped hyena seem much bigger and more dangerous than it actually is.

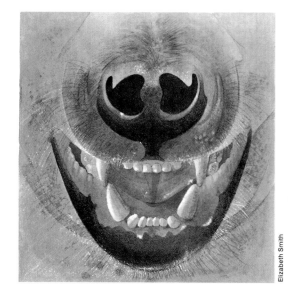

Hyenas range in size from the aardwolf, with a head-and-body length of 22–32 in (55–80 cm), to the spotted hyena, with a head-and-body length of 47–55 in (120–140 cm).

MUZZLE

The strong jaws have powerful muscles attached to a crest on top of the skull. These give the spotted hyena a bone-crushing biting pressure of 11,400 lb/sq in (800 kg/sq cm).

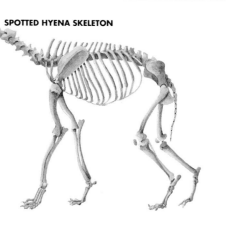

Elizabeth Smith

FEET

The strong feet have sturdy, nonretractile claws like those of a dog, adapted for running fast over grassland.

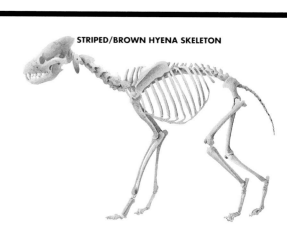

Hyenas have long, powerful, mobile necks, massively developed forequarters and front limbs, sloping backs, and relatively lightly built hindquarters and hind limbs. The emphasis on the front end is reflected in their skeletons.

SPOTTED HYENA SKELETON

STRIPED/BROWN HYENA SKELETON

X-ray illustrations Elizabeth Smith

STRIPED HYENA

In the striped hyena the black stripes on a background of gray or beige may have developed as a form of camouflage.

BROWN HYENA

The white mane of the brown hyena forms a striking contrast with the dark brown hair on its body. The coat is long and coarse.

SPOTTED HYENA

In the spotted hyena the striped coat pattern has become broken up into irregular spots of dark brown on a yellow-white background.

CLASSIFICATION

GENUS: *CROCUTA*

SPECIES: *CROCUTA*

SIZE

HEAD–BODY LENGTH: 4–4.5 FT (120–140 CM)

TAIL LENGTH: 9–12 IN (25–30 CM)

HEIGHT: 2.2–2.9 FT (70–90 CM)

WEIGHT: 110–175 LB (50–80 KG)

WEIGHT AT BIRTH: 3.5 LB (1.5 KG)

ON AVERAGE, FEMALES ARE 12 PERCENT HEAVIER THAN MALES

COLORATION

GRAYISH YELLOW WITH IRREGULAR DARK BROWN SPOTS ON THE BODY. MUZZLE, LOWER LIMBS, AND TAIL BRUSH DARKER

CUBS: DARK GRAYISH BROWN

FEATURES

POWERFUL BUILD, ESPECIALLY FOREQUARTERS

LONG NECK AND SLOPING BACK

HEAVY MUZZLE WITH MASSIVE TEETH

GENITALS OF FEMALE RESEMBLE THOSE OF MALE

THE TAIL

Hyena tails are medium length and bushy (less so in the spotted hyena). The tail hides the anal pouch that lies between the tail and the rectum.

←

↑ *UNDERBELLY*

A hyenid's stomach is very efficient. Scavenging hyenas can digest bones and teeth, and the aardwolf can neutralize the poisonous secretions that make its termite prey inedible to most animals.

Anatomy illustrations Guy Troughton

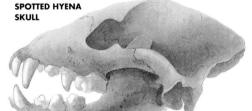

SPOTTED HYENA SKULL

The spotted hyena has an immensely strong skull and jaw; long canines at the front of its mouth are used for ripping and killing, while massive bone-crushing premolars and scissorlike carnassials at the back slice through hide and flesh.

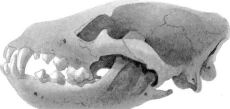

STRIPED HYENA SKULL

The striped hyena has a less massive jaw and a shallower skull crest than the spotted hyena. The premolars and carnassials are adapted for bone cracking, so it is less well equipped for shearing the flesh of live prey.

AARDWOLF SKULL

The termite-eating aardwolf has retained its long canine teeth for fighting, but its redundant cheek teeth have become mere pegs. It uses its lower front incisors as a spade for digging termites out of the earth.

NIGHT PROWLER

AS THE SUN DIPS BELOW THE HORIZON, THE HYENAS START THEIR DAY. SENSES TUNED TO THE TAINT OF DEATH, THEY SET OUT TO SCAVENGE AND KILL

A hyena is a creature of the night. By day it will sprawl for hours in the shelter of a thicket, curled up asleep or lying prone with its nose on its forepaws like a domestic dog. As dusk darkens the savannas and deserts, however, the hyena is transformed. Spotted hyenas in particular are galvanized into activity, snuffling around each other and calling as they stir themselves for the night's work. Then they take off into the twilight, senses alert for the first hint of possible prey or the reek of blood.

Spotted hyenas normally hunt twice a night, in groups. On average, the first phase begins around five o'clock and continues until roughly eight o'clock; a second, shorter phase starts before dawn and may continue for up to two hours after first

Anything is fair game to a hyena. Here they are seen chasing lesser flamingos on Lake Magadi in Tanzania.

WHEN FOOD IS SCARCE, A BROWN HYENA MAY SEARCH ALL NIGHT WITHOUT RESTING, THEN RETURN TO THE SAME DEN

light. This preference for twilight probably reflects the hyena's predatory habits—it is easier to catch your prey if you can see it clearly. The pattern varies, however, depending on where the hyenas are living. The big hyena clans of the Ngorongoro Crater in Tanzania can count on easy pickings from among the large population of resident grazing animals and may forage or hunt for less than three hours. By contrast, the spotted hyenas of the Kalahari have a thinner time of it and may spend more than eight hours on the trail.

Brown and striped hyenas are strictly nocturnal. The striped hyena lies low all day in a cave or in a lair under an uprooted tree and emerges at dusk to forage for carrion or small live prey. It may keep going until midnight, then rest for several hours before starting again. By daybreak it has gone to shelter again, but not necessarily in the same place.

Johnathan Scott/Planet Earth Pictures

Striped hyenas that have been radio-tracked in the Serengeti rarely use the same lair more than two days running.

Bob Campbell/Survival Anglia

Johnathan Scott/PEP

Spotted hyenas are the largest of the hyena species and would kill other hyenas to possess a carcass.

Both the striped and brown hyenas tend to live in arid regions where food is often scarce. In many areas they also find themselves in competition with the bigger spotted hyena and have little opportunity to share the big kills. Since the food they find is often barely adequate for one, the striped and brown hyenas generally forage alone, zigzagging over wide areas, but they live in family groups.

The aardwolf is the most nocturnal of all hyenids. The termites that form most of its diet are active at night, so the aardwolf has to seek them out at that time. Although it typically lives in pairs, it forages alone—there is no advantage in cooperative hunting for such prey, and since the termites are erratic in their behavior, it is more efficient for the pair to hunt separately. An aardwolf may spend six hours a night on its quest, and when a pair is breeding they take turns defending the cubs. ■

SHARING THE SPOILS

Hyenas are not the only scavengers on the plains of Africa and southern Asia. Any carcass they find is likely to attract a host of species including jackals, vultures, marabou storks, wild dogs, and lions.

Competition over a kill is unwelcome, but hyenas are more tolerant of some predators than others. Jackals often nip in to grab a mouthful without being attacked, but hyenas regularly drive lions away from their kills and occasionally kill young lions—but then lions will often reverse this situation. Normally it is the outnumbered animals that retreat.

HABITATS

Evolution has endowed hyenas with tremendous stamina, and despite their awkward appearance they can travel great distances without apparent fatigue. They have sturdy legs and toes with strong, nonretractile claws like those of a dog, adapted for running over level ground, and these factors make them well suited to life in open country, where food is often widely scattered.

The counterpart of the striped hyena in the south is the brown hyena, which occurs in southern Africa south of the Zambezi. These two species are much the same size and have very similar habits. It is significant that their ranges do not overlap: scavenging is a competitive trade, and two such equally matched rivals would probably spend their lives fighting if they were close neighbors.

The central and southern African range of the spotted hyena, however, overlaps those of both the

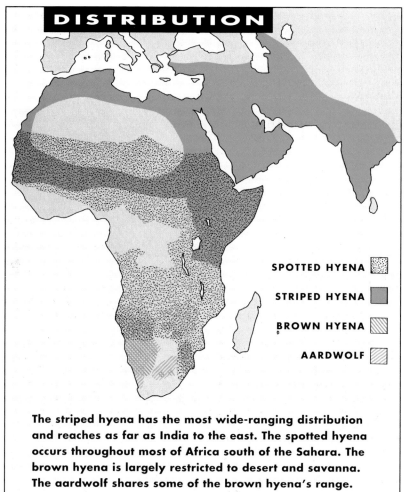

DISTRIBUTION

SPOTTED HYENA

STRIPED HYENA

BROWN HYENA

AARDWOLF

The striped hyena has the most wide-ranging distribution and reaches as far as India to the east. The spotted hyena occurs throughout most of Africa south of the Sahara. The brown hyena is largely restricted to desert and savanna. The aardwolf shares some of the brown hyena's range.

Johnathan Scott/Planet Earth Pictures

The pickings are rich for the spotted hyena during the calving season of the wildebeest.

others. Much bigger, and a killer as well as a scavenger, the spotted hyena's requirements are slightly different from those of its smaller relatives, so it can live alongside them in relative harmony. It will not hesitate to attack either in a confrontation, but there are sufficient alternatives available to make this a relatively rare event.

In particular, the spotted hyena concentrates on the larger herbivores that, in some areas, still teem on the African savanna. The largest populations of spotted hyenas occur on the east African plains of Kenya and Tanzania, in the game reserves of the Masai Mara, the Serengeti, and Ngorongoro, where wildebeests and zebras still roam in the thousands.

The savanna is a sea of grass, dotted with trees

Clem Haagner/Ardea

such as the great spreading acacias and the strange baobab, with its swollen, water-storing trunk. Water is at a premium on the savanna, because rain falls only during the rainy season from November to April; for the rest of the year it is hot and arid.

For the grazing animals, this seasonal cycle is crucial. In the dry season the grasses hardly grow at all, and in most areas the animals must keep moving to find suitable food. In the Serengeti, this continu-

> THE AARDWOLF HAS A MOBILE TONGUE THAT CAN ROLL UP COMPLETELY WHEN IT CLEANS ITS MOUTH CAVITY

ous movement develops into a full-scale migration in May, when the herds finally exhaust the pasture in the dry southeast section of the reserve. Following some ancestral instinct, they head for the Mara in southern Kenya, where the grasses are still lush and green. By November they have exhausted the Mara, too, but by then the rains have brought a flush of green to the southern savannas, so the herds retrace their steps to the Serengeti.

These movements are naturally of the greatest interest to spotted hyenas, which prey on the grazing animals or scavenge their carcasses. So from November to May, when the herds are grazing the Serengeti, hundreds of hyenas feed within the reserve. When the herds move north, the Serengeti hyenas are left with no food supply except small

Clem Haagner/Ardea

Spotted hyenas at den site (left). *This is the time to stretch, scratch, and groom themselves like cats.*

A brown hyena (above) *in the Kalahari picks over the bones of another animal's kill.*

KEY FACTS

● The spotted hyena is the most abundant large carnivore in Africa today. Of no use to humans, it is not hunted for its fur or other properties like the big cats.

● The aardwolf prefers to live on grassland that has been overgrazed by hoofed animals such as wildebeests and gazelles, because the very short grass provides an ideal habitat for the harvester termites it preys upon.

● On the coast of Namibia the brown hyena is known as a beach wolf or beachcomber because of its habit of scavenging along the beachfront debris washed up by the tide.

● The striped hyena is the most widely distributed of all the hyenas, but it occurs at very low densities and is endangered in North Africa.

game. They cannot move north without trespassing on the territory of other hyenas, so they tend to make temporary forays, returning every day or so to the clan den.

Brown hyenas have a similar problem in the southwest arid zone of Africa, which includes the Kalahari and Namib Deserts. During the rainy season a host of grazing animals—wildebeests, red hartebeests, and springboks—migrate into the central Kalahari. They are accompanied by the lions, cheetahs, and spotted hyenas that prey on them, and the brown hyenas, being primarily scavengers, enjoy rich pickings from these kills. When the rains stop, the herds leave, but instead of chasing them the brown hyenas switch to a less ambitious diet of small vertebrates, insects, and fruits, which provide vital moisture during the dry months in the desert. In the Kalahari the animals may have to roam 30 miles (50 km) a night to get enough to eat.

In the far west of their range, on the edge of the Namib Desert, brown hyenas avoid this problem by scavenging along the beachfront of the Skeleton Coast. Here their diet is seasonally enriched by the mass breeding of the Cape fur seals, which haul out in vast colonies on the beaches. These colonies

offer unlimited food for a few months, after which the brown hyenas may have to make do with dead seabirds, fish, and marine debris.

The striped hyena is a solitary scavenger and small-time hunter. It will eat almost anything including carrion, small vertebrates, eggs, insects, and fruits. It will take advantage of the big kills if it can, but more typically it ranges widely in search of smaller prey and scraps, sometimes picking over garbage dumps. This enables it to survive in some of the most barren country of all. ■

FOCUS ON

HYENAS IN THE NGORONGORO

The Ngorongoro Crater in Tanzania is shaped like a gigantic circular dish. Its rim completely surrounds an area of rich grassland, which, feeds a variety of animals. The big animals that live on the crater floor can migrate in and out of the crater, but they often stay all year round.

About 25,000 hoofed grazing animals live within the crater. These make rich pickings for the lions and spotted hyenas that prey on them. The hyenas, some 400 of them, outnumber the lions three to one, and as a result they have become the major predators. This means that instead of scavenging lion kills, the hyenas generally kill their own prey and the lions do the scavenging—when they get the chance. The hyenas often hunt in packs of twenty or more, so although a pride of lions may win temporary possession of a carcass, the hyenas usually drive them away.

RAINFALL

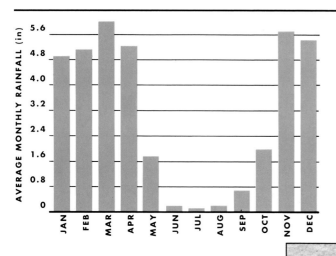

During the rainy season from October to April, the grasslands are lush and green. In the driest months from July to September, the grasses scorch in the hot sun, making life difficult for the grazing animals that have to scratch a living anywhere they can.

NEIGHBORS

The Ngorongoro Crater supports a variety of wildlife. The largest grazers are the wildebeests and the largest predators are the lions.

PLAINS ZEBRA

Living in small groups, the plains zebras occupy a territory of 30–100 sq mi (80–250 sq km) in the crater.

ELAND

Elands are spiral-horned antelope that often form large groups, especially in the breeding season.

All illustrations Wayne Ford/Wildlife Art Agency

ENEMIES

THE NGORONGORO CRATER

Situated in Tanzania, the Ngorongoro Crater rim stands about 2,300 ft (700 m) high and is 11 miles (18 km) across. The crater is actually a caldera—the collapsed, eroded remains of a vast, extinct volcano.

Map labels: KENYA, Lake Victoria, MARA, Mabalageti, TANZANIA, Simiyu, Lake Natron, Loolmasalin Mountain, Ngorongoro Crater, Lake Eyasi, Lake Manyana

Kilometers
0 40 80
0 20 40
Miles

EXTREMELY DANGEROUS

LION
A fierce competitor of the hyena, skirmishes often take place between them. Each will kill the other.

MODERATELY DANGEROUS

AFRICAN BUFFALO
Although hyenas feed on the remains of buffalo killed by other animals, they rarely attack this large, dangerous beast themselves.

THOMSON'S GAZELLE

About 90 percent of this gazelle's food is grass. It is an abundant species and a favorite prey of hyenas.

VULTURE

Quick to spot a kill, vultures wait for the predator to take its fill before stepping in to pick the bones clean.

COMMON JACKAL

Jackals live in small family units that hunt as a team. They often steal from hyenas and lions.

SOUTHERN REEDBUCK

A characteristic of the reedbuck is its leaping into the air when running. This species is the largest.

WILDEBEEST

The wildebeest, or gnu, has a relatively massive head and shoulders. Both sexes have horns.

SOCIAL STRUCTURE

With their undeniable talent for slaughter and butchery, hyenas might seem ill-equipped for civilized society. Yet their social systems are among the most complex and subtle known among carnivores and certainly far more sophisticated than those of their prey. This is partly a consequence of their notorious savagery. Such lethal creatures are obviously a potential threat to each other, and a dispute could easily escalate into a murderous fight. In the short term this might help the victor, but in the long term it would eliminate hyena social structure. Accordingly hyenas have evolved social codes for avoiding the ultimate confrontation, and in spotted hyenas these systems are the foundation of a cooperative, pack-hunting society.

The basis of hyena society is communication—by sound, sight, touch, and scent. Spotted hyenas in particular are extremely vocal, with 11 different types of calls. Their repertoire includes the notorious manic giggle, which is actually an expression of fear.

By contrast, the brown and striped hyenas are quite restrained in their vocalization, and the aardwolf is virtually silent. But they communicate visually using facial expressions and body language.

All hyenas scent-mark their territory liberally, and these secretions provide other hyenas with information about the individual's clan, sex, sexual state, and activities. Direct sniffing is also important: Brown and striped hyenas protrude their anal pouches when they meet

MATRIARCH

In spotted hyenas, the females rule the clan. They are heavier than the males and more aggressive. Even the cubs are aggressive.

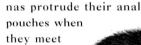

DEFENSE

With tail erect and mane bristling, a resident spotted hyena intimidates a trespasser.

"KISSING"

A young spotted hyena may greet an unrelated adult female by "kissing" her on the muzzle.

FEAR GRIMACE

An intimidated brown hyena grimaces in fear—a submissive expression designed to avert aggression.

ERECT MANE

A striped hyena erects its mane to give an enemy the impression that it is bigger than it really is.

WHOOP CALL

Head lowered, a spotted hyena gives the rising whoop call to communicate with other clan members.

GENITAL SNIFF

Spotted hyenas greet each other face-to-face, then turn and sniff each others' genitals in a display of mutual trust.

in SIGHT

CONFUSION

Female spotted hyenas not only dominate the males, they look like them too. The female's genitalia mimics the male's, so the two sexes are almost indistinguishable. This has probably come about because the females have high levels of male hormones in their blood. These make them bigger and more aggressive than they would otherwise be, allowing them to dominate males at a kill. This way they acquire enough nutrition to nurse their cubs. But a side effect of the high male hormone level is the development of masculine behavior patterns.

and present them to each other for inspection.

Among brown and striped hyenas, breeding females and young live in small clans with low-status, nonbreeding males and females, while dominant males tend to roam alone and mate with the clan females. The males are slightly heavier than the females, and they are more aggressive.

Spotted hyenas live in large clans, with many breeding females sharing a communal den. The females are bigger than the males and dominate them socially; indeed the whole clan is led by a single dominant female, and there is a definite order of precedence. The offspring of high-ranking females have high status themselves within the clan, and it is these male offspring that stand the best chance of being accepted into other clans, where they mate with the resident females. ■

HUNTING

All hyenas scavenge, but only spotted hyenas habitually hunt large animals. In some areas such as the Ngorongoro Crater, they get nearly all their food in this way, behaving more like wolves than the popular image of the hyena.

A spotted hyena will hunt alone for small prey such as a Thomson's gazelle, but bringing down bigger quarry usually takes cooperation. This is possible because of the tight social structure of the clan, which enables the hyenas to communicate almost telepathically.

The clan normally splits into several smaller packs to go hunting. The size of the pack depends on the prey: Two or three hyenas can cope with a wildebeest, for example, but a zebra hunt usually involves a pack of ten or more. Once the pack has made a kill, other members of the clan—particularly high-ranking females—may stroll up to share the

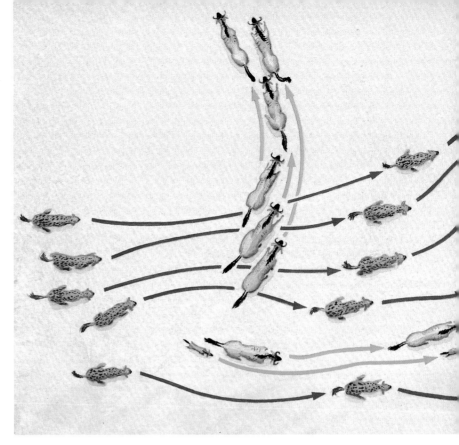

THE TACTICS
Having selected their target, the hyenas ignore the rest of the herd, which veers away to the left.
They then cut off the victim's retreat.

THE SNATCH
A gang of spotted hyenas snatch a wildebeest calf from under its mother's nose.

PREY

Spotted hyenas will eat anything that is presented to them, however large. An adult wildebeest is stripped to the bone in fifteen minutes by a pack—the bones take a little longer.

WARTHOG

FLAMINGO

Illustrations Craig Douglas/Wildlife Art Agency

feast, pushing aside those that did the hunting.

Hyenas rely on stamina to catch their prey. As they approach, their quarry usually takes flight and the hyenas settle down to a long chase. Before long one of the prey animals—usually an old, sick, or very young individual—may lag behind the others, and the hyenas single it out for attack. They split up, some running wide to outflank the fugitive if it veers off to one side. Eventually one may grab it by its muzzle or tail, and the rest pile all over it, knocking it over and ripping its stomach out to kill it.

These tactics are among the most efficient of all carnivores, but the success rate is only some 30 to 40 percent. Two out of three chases end in failure, normally because the quarry outruns the pack. If

THE KILL

Once one hyena gets a grip on the nose or tail, the others rush in for the kill.

the prey animals keep together they stand a good chance of escape, and zebras will improve the odds by lashing out with their hooves. A wildebeest will sometimes turn and threaten its pursuers with its sharp horns, but this simply gives other hyenas the chance to surround it and pull it down.

The hyenas are most successful during the breeding season. Wildebeest calves in particular are easy meat, and the hyenas often hunt in daylight at this time of year. In some areas up to three-quarters of the season's calves may be devoured by hyenas, but the wildebeest produce so many over such a short period that the hyenas cannot eat them all. This is known as synchronized breeding; many calves at one time overwhelm the predators and increase overall calf survival.

After the kill the hyenas eat fast. The feast is confused and noisy, with each hyena fighting for its share, although the dominant females usually make out best. Individual hyenas often run off with bloody fragments of the carcass to devour them in peace or bury them for later; spotted hyenas will often cache food in muddy pools, returning for them when they are hungry. Nothing is wasted, and the attendant jackals often go hungry. ∎

in SIGHT

THE ZEBRA HUNT

Occasionally spotted hyenas seem to set out with the deliberate intention of hunting zebras. A pack of up to twenty-five will gather together and lope away over the savanna under the leadership of a high-ranking female, ignoring wildebeests, gazelles, and other distractions until they reach a herd of feeding zebras.

Zebras are not easy prey. The stallions defend their families by kicking and trampling, and the herds stick together and run fast. The hyenas risk being injured or even killed, and they are likely to expend a lot of energy in the hunt. So why bother, when there is easier prey available? No one knows, but perhaps they taste better.

AFRICAN BUFFALO	ORYX	RHINO CALF	WILDEBEEST	THOMSON'S GAZELLE	ZEBRA

TERRITORY

The size and nature of a hyena's territory depends on its social arrangements and the availability of food. In the Ngorongoro, food is plentiful throughout the year, and the resident spotted hyenas do not have to range far to find it. Large clans of 35–80 hyenas occupy relatively small, permanent territories averaging 12 sq miles (30 sq km). The bigger the clan, the bigger the territory, and the boundaries are scent marked regularly and fiercely defended against interlopers.

Compared with most hyenas, the Ngorongoro clans live in luxury. They can afford to defend exclusive territories because, food being plentiful, they never have to forage beyond them. Elsewhere in Africa the situation is often very different. In the southern Kalahari, for example, spotted hyenas find life hard. Large prey is scarce, live or dead, and the hyenas range over huge areas of up to 775 sq miles (2,000 sq km) in small groups of 3–12 individuals. Such an area is impossible to defend effectively, and indeed such defense would be pointless; each clan takes the freedom to roam where it will to find sufficient food. Under these circumstances, interconflict is not worth the investment of energy and potential injury.

A large foraging area of this type is known as a home range, to distinguish it from the hyena's

ANAL POUCH

A hyena's main scent-marking device is its anal pouch, which lies just beneath its tail. The lining of the pouch can be forced out like a balloon, and when the hyena wants to leave its mark, it straddles a suitably sturdy grass stalk and works it into the groove in the center of the inflated pouch, smearing it with a strong-smelling paste.

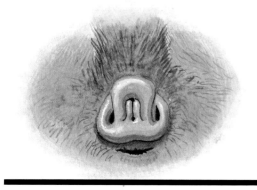

defended territory, which often lies near the center of the foraging area and includes its breeding den. But sometimes the territory and the feeding area are widely separated, particularly in regions where the prey animals are migratory.

In the Serengeti, spotted hyenas have fixed territories, but their prey migrates north to find fresh pasture in the dry season. So the Serengeti clans establish dens near the northern boundaries of their territories and embark on a series of cross-border raids into the adjoining territories to the north. This banditry is tolerated but it is exhausting; the Serengeti hyenas may travel 19 miles (30 km) each way, day after day, throughout the dry season. In southern Botswana similar migrations force the spotted hyenas to commute up to 50 miles (80 km) each way, and the hunters may be away from the den for five days or more. Since spotted hyenas leave their cubs unattended while they hunt, many die of starvation or are killed by predators.

Hyenas scent mark with their anal glands throughout their territories, and they may also do so when they range farther afield. The terrain nearer the den is crossed more frequently, so it is marked even more strongly.

CLAN MARKINGS

The range map shows anal scent marks deposited in a year by five adult brown hyenas. Note that the marking density is highest in the central parts of the range, around water sources, food caches, dens, and well-used trails, but the borders of the territory are defined by a perimeter "fence" of marks.

SCENT MARKING

Crouching down on its haunches,
a brown hyena scent marks a
grass stem with the secretion from
its anal pouch.

Scent marking has two functions. First, it supplies other hyenas with information; if they are clan members they will know who has been where. Second, it has a direct effect on the confidence of residents and trespassers. A hyena within its territory is surrounded by familiar scents and is secure of its position. A trespasser, by contrast, is surrounded by unfamiliar scents, and although it may act bravely, its confidence level is often close to zero. If there is a confrontation it will almost certainly turn tail and run. But when the fugitive picks up the familiar scents of home, its confidence returns, and it may turn snarling on its pursuer. Eventually there is a stalemate at the point where the levels of insecurity are exactly balanced: the territorial boundary.

To some extent this is an automatic phenomenon, but hyenas may occasionally turn it to their advantage. The brown hyenas of the Skeleton Coast, for example, often range far into the barren Namib Desert for no apparent reason. There is no food there, or at least nothing that can compare with the riches to be found along the coastal strand. It is possible, however, that the hyenas make the trip with the sole object of "claiming" a buffer zone of desert by scent marking to put off trespassers. ■

AARDWOLF

The habitat and territory of the aardwolf is determined by its specialized diet. The harvester termites it prefers feed mainly among the well-grazed grassland of the African savannas, and they are often extremely abundant, emerging from their mounds at night to forage in long columns of 5,000 or so. A pair of aardwolves and their young can generally find enough to eat within a small territory; they will scent mark and defend this resolutely and chase away intruders.

In winter, harvester termites stay underground, for they are unable to operate on cold winter nights and cannot survive exposure to sunshine. The aardwolves have to switch to a hardier species, but they do less well on the diet and may lose a quarter of their body weight during the colder months. At such times the territorial system may break down as neighboring animals search for scarce prey.

The aardwolf rests during the day in cool caves.
It hunts at night for harvester termites.

LIFE CYCLE

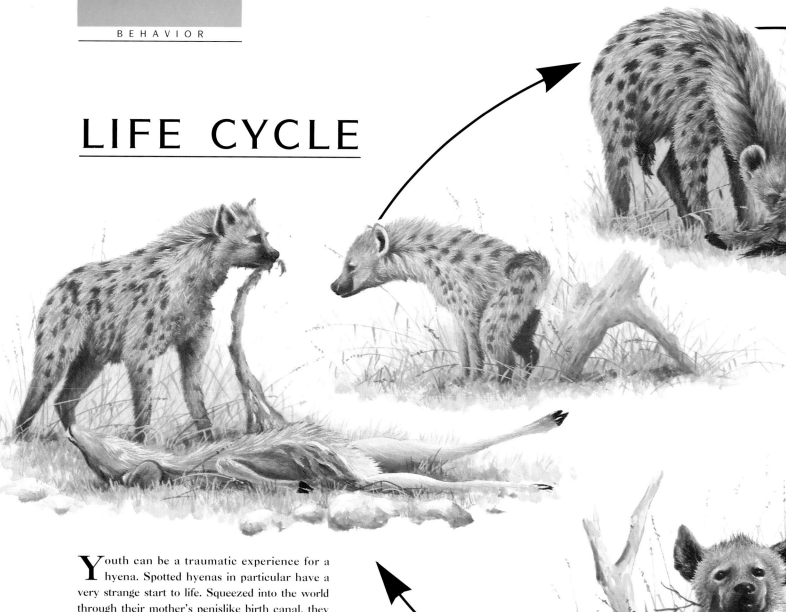

Youth can be a traumatic experience for a hyena. Spotted hyenas in particular have a very strange start to life. Squeezed into the world through their mother's penislike birth canal, they emerge fully furred, with their eyes open, a set of sharp teeth, and an instinctive ferocity that is unique among mammals. A new born spotted hyena will fall upon its brother or sister, grab it by the neck, and shake it, exactly as its mother will shake a gazelle fawn to kill it. The intention is equally murderous, and a quarter of all cubs starve to death because siblings bully them out of their share of milk.

The result is that only the strongest survive. But they need to be strong, for their mothers may leave

WEANING

After a few days without milk, the yearling cubs start to follow the adults as they forage and to learn how to find food for themselves.

Clem Haagner/Ardea

in SIGHT

GENETIC INTEREST

All the females in a spotted hyena clan breed if they can. In clans of brown hyenas, only one female breeds and all the adults in the clan help take care of the cubs, bringing food back to the den for them. The helping adults are usually older siblings or other close relatives, making the cubs a good "genetic investment."

GROWING UP

The life of a young hyena

Illustration John Morris/Wildlife Art Agency

COURTSHIP

Courtship can be a hazardous process for a male spotted hyena, for the female is often aggressive. Even if she accepts his advances, she may change her mind if a bigger, stronger male appears.

MATING

A successful courtship culminates in mating— a complicated process in which the male has to probe right underneath the female to penetrate her fully retracted sexual organs.

SUCKLING

Spotted hyenas raise their cubs communally in a clan den, but each mother suckles her own cubs. The cubs may feed for over an hour at a time.

FROM BIRTH TO DEATH

SPOTTED HYENA
GESTATION: 110 DAYS
LITTER SIZE: 1–2
BREEDING: NONSEASONAL
WEIGHT AT BIRTH: 3.5 LB (1.5 KG)
EYES OPEN: AT BIRTH

WEANING: 12–16 MONTHS
HUNTING: 18 MONTHS
SEXUAL MATURITY: 2 YEARS FOR MALES, 3 YEARS FOR FEMALES
LONGEVITY: 25 YEARS IN WILD, 41 YEARS IN CAPTIVITY

BROWN HYENA
GESTATION: 90 DAYS
LITTER SIZE: 2–5
BREEDING: NONSEASONAL
WEIGHT AT BIRTH: 1.5 LB (770 G)

EYES OPEN: 8 DAYS
WEANING: 6 MONTHS
FORAGING: 14 MONTHS
SEXUAL MATURITY: 2–3 YEARS
LONGEVITY: 24 YEARS IN CAPTIVITY

them for days at a time to go hunting. When the females return they call the cubs out of the den—an abandoned aardvark burrow or similar tunnel system—and suckle them, often for an hour or more at a time. Spotted hyena adults never bring solid food to their young, so the cubs are fed entirely on milk for at least nine months.

Eventually the milk supply dries up, to the displeasure of the young hyenas, who throw tantrums and may even bite at their mothers. Eventually they accept the situation and start tagging along on the hunt, but they can only hunt effectively on their own at the age of about eighteen months. Meanwhile they learn scent marking and social skills through

play, and at puberty the young males leave the clan to try their luck elsewhere.

Young females usually stay within the clan and solicit the attentions of roving males. Being smaller and less aggressive, a male has to work hard at courtship, and he will often grovel before a female to appease her. After some days of this she may accept him, but she may switch her attention to another male of higher rank. Such status is closely associated with strength and aggression, and she instinctively looks for these qualities in the animal that will sire her cubs. ■

TREATED AS VERMIN

WIDELY DESPISED AS MALEVOLENT SCAVENGERS, HYENAS HAVE FEW FRIENDS AND MUST RELY ON THEIR OWN ADAPTABILITY TO SURVIVE IN A LARGELY HOSTILE WORLD

When the European settlers began working their way north through Africa from the Cape in the 19th century, they entered a natural paradise. The plains were alive with animals: zebras, wildebeest, hartebeest, eland, gazelles, springbok, blesbok, gemsbok, and many, many more, grazing in vast herds stretching to the grassy horizons.

These herds were preyed upon by a fearsome assortment of predators and scavengers including lions, cheetahs, leopards, wild dogs, jackals, and of course hyenas. The predators were always far less numerous than their prey, since it takes many plant-eaters to sustain one meat-eater, but the sheer mass of animals grazing the African plains was sufficient to support large, flourishing populations of carnivores.

Within a century, however, most of the great grazing herds had disappeared—shot for sport or

---

IN EAST AFRICA THE MASAI LAY
OUT THEIR DEAD FOR THE
SPOTTED HYENAS TO DISPOSE OF

---

to make way for the colonists' cattle—and as their food supply dwindled, so did the carnivores. Many populations simply faded away. The more imposing predators often fell victim to the big-game hunters, for whom a dead lion or leopard was the ultimate trophy. The hyenas, however, fared even worse.

Owing to the popular image of hyenas as craven scavengers, the big-game hunters and general public had no interest in them, but to the farmers they were vermin. All hyenas—except the termite-eating aardwolf—will kill domestic livestock if they get the chance, and a big clan of spotted hyenas will make short work of a herd of

cattle or a flock of sheep. As a result they were shot, trapped, and poisoned like rats, with the aim of eradicating them completely.

In many areas this aim has been achieved. The spotted and brown hyenas have been exterminated from much of their former ranges in southern Africa, and the brown hyena has retreated to the arid lands of the Kalahari and Namib Deserts in Botswana and Namibia. It is still relatively widespread in this inhospitable terrain, but at low densities. To survive in the Kalahari a clan of four or five brown hyenas must range over a vast territory of 120 sq miles (300 sq km) or more during the dry

Top predators of the Ngorongoro Crater in Tanzania, the spotted hyenas are reduced to scavenging from garbage dumps in South Africa.

Peter Pickford/NHPA

Peter Johnson/NHPA

In some parts of their range, spotted hyenas often lose out to lions and have to bide their time.

This chart shows the Kalahari and the amount of brown hyenas it could support.

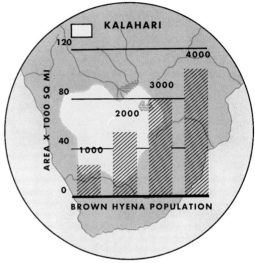

KALAHARI

BROWN HYENA POPULATION

The average clan size of brown hyenas is made up of four or five animals. They spend more time searching for food than spotted hyenas because the food is so widely scattered. On average they travel about 20 miles (30 km) over a ten-hour period each day in search of food. Given that each clan needs 120 sq miles (300 sq km), the Kalahari could support about 4,000 animals.

season, so it takes an immense tract of land to support a population of 500 or so—the minimum number necessary for long-term survival.

During the rainy season brown hyenas benefit from the migrations of grazing animals into the Kalahari to feed on the temporary flush of growth, but they are discouraged from following the herds back into the richer grasslands by competition with the bigger, stronger spotted hyenas. So they tend to stay in the deserts.

The highest densities of brown hyenas are found in the Kalahari and Gemsbok National Parks, where they are protected. Elsewhere they are still regularly killed, and the species is officially listed as vulnerable.

By comparison, the striped hyena has a huge range, but it may be equally threatened. It was once a relatively common scavenger around areas of human habitation, but it can be destructive to crops such as melons, peaches, dates, and grapes, as well as to livestock. Inevitably it has been persecuted and driven into the mountains and desert fringes. Like the brown hyena, it has a talent for surviving in such arid terrain, but only at low densities, and its numbers appear to be very much reduced. The North African race is classified as endangered, which means that it may soon be extinct.

The spotted hyena can also live off scraps, but essentially it is a predator and scavenger of large and medium-sized hoofed animals. Today the great

---

**A SINGLE SPOTTED HYENA
CAN GULP DOWN A GAZELLE FAWN
IN TWO MINUTES**

---

herds of grazing animals are more or less restricted to parks and reserves such as the Serengeti and Masai Mara; the hyenas flourish in these protected zones—although they were originally treated as vermin and dealt with accordingly. Beyond the reserve boundaries they are still persecuted and becoming rare, but despite this the species as a whole is in no immediate danger.

This leaves the aardwolf: a timid, harmless termite eater, incapable of killing livestock and quite indifferent to fruit and other crops. Yet even the aardwolf is shot on occasion, sometimes because it is assumed to be a predator and sometimes for its fur or meat, which is considered a delicacy by some. A more important problem is habitat loss,

HYENAS IN DANGER

THE CHART BELOW SHOWS HOW, IN **1990**, THE INTERNATIONAL UNION FOR THE CONSERVATION OF NATURE (IUCN), OR THE WORLD CONSERVATION UNION, CLASSIFIED THE CONSERVATION STATUS OF THE HYENAS.

BROWN HYENA	**VULNERABLE**
STRIPED HYENA	**CITES** LISTED

VULNERABLE MEANS THAT THE SPECIES IS LIKELY TO DECLINE AND BECOME SERIOUSLY ENDANGERED IF NOTHING IS DONE TO IMPROVE ITS SITUATION. *CITES LISTED* MEANS THAT THE SPECIES IS NOT CONSIDERED SUFFICIENTLY AT RISK TO BE ON THE DANGER LIST OF THE **IUCN**, BUT IT IS LISTED BY THE CONVENTION ON INTERNATIONAL TRADE IN ENDANGERED SPECIES (OF WILD FLOWER AND FAUNA).

THE SPOTTED HYENA AND THE AARDWOLF ARE NOT LISTED BY EITHER ORGANIZATION.

but currently the aardwolf remains numerous throughout its range.

The aardwolf has survived for thousands of years because it has specialized in a prey that attracts little interest from other species—including humans. But for the other hyenids, their way of life brings them into direct conflict with humans, so ultimately their long-term survival is at our discretion. ∎

A hyena being released, just in time, from a cruel wire snare.

Topham Picture Source

Peter Pickford/NHPA

ALONGSIDE MAN

BAD REPUTATION

The bad reputation of hyenas is mainly because their scavenging habits are seen as filthy, squalid, and somehow cowardly. Throughout history humans have admired murderous predators such as lions and tigers but despised the scavengers that clean up after them.

Our primitive ancestors were probably living much like hyenas on the plains of Africa: stealing the kills of other predators, scavenging scraps, and killing when they could. For such people the destructive power of a lion was enviable but the scavenging skills of a hyena simply made it a hated competitor. This attitude may have passed down through the generations and been justified by tales of grave robbing, child snatching, and other loathsome habits.

INTO THE FUTURE

As big carnivores, hyenas belong to the group of animals that has probably suffered most at the hands of man. Carnivores represent a threat—both to people and to their livestock—so throughout history they have been ruthlessly hunted down and destroyed. In many parts of the world animals such as wolves, lions, and bears have been exterminated from areas where they were formerly common, and the same thing has happened to spotted and brown hyenas throughout most of South Africa. However formidable the species—and the spotted hyena is one of the most powerful predators on Earth—it is no match for a farmer's rifle.

PREDICTION

GAME RESERVES

Adapted as a pack hunter, the spotted hyena needs access to big concentrations of game animals. Before long these will be restricted to wildlife reserves and the spotted hyena will then become dependent on man's whims.

Yet hyenas have a factor in their favor: They are opportunists, ready to eat more or less anything, and this enables them to survive in the most inhospitable environments—places that are quite unsuited to agriculture and raising stock, and rarely visited by man. So although the brown hyena, for example, has been wiped out from the farming country of South Africa, it still thrives in the Namib and Kalahari Deserts. It is greatly reduced and officially listed as vulnerable, but since it poses no threat to man's activities, it could survive indefinitely. ∎

FINANCIAL RUIN

J. B. Davidson/Survival Anglia

The greatest threat to the spotted hyena is the development of livestock ranching within its core habitats, the savannas of east and south Africa. Attempts to raise cattle in many of these areas have been discouraged by the aridity of the terrain and plagues of parasites such as the tsetse fly, but these problems may be overcome by domesticating native animals such as the eland.

Such concepts are still in the experimental stage, but if they become commercially viable the unprotected savannas will become economically valuable, and native predators such as the spotted hyena will be driven out.

NATURAL ADVANTAGES

The African savanna reserves are now the only grasslands in the world that still support near-natural populations of grazing animals and big predators such as lions, cheetahs, and hyenas. Because of this they are a unique attraction for tourists and are now a major source of foreign revenue in many African countries, outperforming many more conventional forms of trade. Consequently it may be economically advantageous to extend the reserves and encourage the types of animals that have been wiped out—hyenas included.

Illustration Phillip Hood

INDEX

Published by Marshall Cavendish Corporation
99 White Plains Road
Tarrytown, New York 10591-9001

© Marshall Cavendish Corporation, 1997
© Marshall Cavendish Ltd, 1994

The material in this series was first published in the English language by Marshall Cavendish Limited, of 119 Wardour Street, London W1V 3TD, England.

Library of Congress Cataloging-in-Publication Data

Encyclopedia of mammals.
    p. cm.
    Includes index.
    ISBN 0-7614-0575-5 (set)   ISBN 0-7614-0582-8 (v. 7)

    Summary: Detailed articles cover the history, anatomy, feeding habits, social structure, reproduction, territory,
        and current status of ninety-five mammals around the world.
    1. Mammals—Encyclopedias, Juvenile. [1. Mammals—Encyclopedias.] I. Marshall Cavendish Corporation.
    QL706.2.E54 1996
    599'.003—dc20
                                                                        96-17736
                                                                           CIP
                                                                           AC

Printed in Malaysia
Bound in U.S.A.